WHAT YOU SAW
...and What You Didn't

*The Stories Behind 50 Years of Broadcast Journalism
and What You Can Learn From Them*

ROSS BECKER

With a foreword by CBS News Correspondent Kris Van Cleave

Book Dedication

For my wife and family, who lived it with me, and for the photojournalists and editors, who shared the pain and glory.

What You Saw...and What You Didn't
The Stories Behind 50 Years of Broadcast Journalism
and What You Can Learn From Them

©2024 Ross Becker

ISBN: 979-8-35094-945-2

CONTENTS

Foreword 1

Preface 3

My First "Real" Job in Broadcast Journalism 7

One Moment in Time 11

The Blue-Eyed Traitor 16

A Very Close Call 21

RIDE, Sally Ride 25

I Interviewed O. J. and No One Saw It! 28

The Energy of a Monster 35

Jelly on a Spoon 38

Mud and Fire and Death 40

Mickey and the Mustard Stain 43

An Ominous Note on the Windshield 45

80 Miles an Hour in the Dark 49

A Beige Gremlin and a Big Decision about Life 53

A Burning Cross and a Party of Hate 58

A Horrible Halloween 62

An Explosion of Emotion 67

Biscuits and Gravy 70

Don't Confuse Me with the Facts 73

Flying Blind 76

Frozen by Fire 80

Jesus or Superman? 84

My Friend, the Murderer 87

A Red, White, and Blue Diaper 90

Right Place, Wrong Time 94

Who Is "Rose Baker"? .97

Running toward the Danger 101

Satanic Panic and a Mexican Standoff 105

The Feeling of Evil 110

A Prayer and a $20 Bill 114

At a Loss for Words 118

Buried in the Snow 121

Don't Ever Ask a Question 125

"Hail Satan!" 129

In the Middle of a Grieving Mob 132

The Government Was Listening 136

Too Tired to Be Scared 139

Sneaking Back into the U.S. 142

You Gotta Have Trust 145

The Sound of Despair 148

The Note Behind the Photograph 152

The Big One that Got Away 155

Final Reflections 159

FOREWORD

by Kris Van Cleave, CBS News National Correspondent

I first met Ross Becker when I was an eager 13-year-old working on a school project about a profession I was interested in. He invited me down to the Los Angeles TV station where he was the main news anchor and talked to me for hours. Looking back on it 30 years later, I realize that was the day when the seeds of much of what I know about journalism were planted.

"When we do our jobs right, journalists are a mirror that reflects the community back upon itself. They won't always like what they see, but that doesn't mean they shouldn't see it looking back at them," Ross told me. It was a simple observation about journalism that has stayed with me story after story and year after year. At the time I didn't realize how often that mirror showed people at their best and at their worst—in both, times of great success and times of great loss.

The stories of great success are uplifting, but more common are the days centered around a great loss. You learn to compartmentalize the trauma of breaking news. I remember telling myself many times: you aren't covering a war, you aren't in combat, just cover the story and go home. For the most part, it worked for me covering shootings, natural disasters, and all the other horrible moments of loss. Some would stay with you: accompanying an Army wife to pick up her husband's remains after his helicopter was shot down in Iraq; the overwhelming and pervasive sadness that hung over the families of the lives taken by a gunman on the campus of Virginia Tech; the profound loss that blanketed a small German town that lost 16 students and two teachers in a horrifying plane crash. While these memories continue to visit my mind, they rarely linger and it's on to the next story.

But January 6, 2021, was different. I was on the west lawn as an angry mob descended upon the United States Capitol, fought with the police, and tore at the fibers of our democracy. Maybe it was because it was happening to the city I called home, maybe it was the fact that, at points, my team and I feared for our safety, or perhaps it was the totality of that moment . . . that history was unfolding around us. I'd covered protests and unrest before, but this was different. Moments from that day haunted me for months.

Years of covering other people's trauma finally hit home. The idea that it could somehow be cumulative hadn't occurred to me. We never talked about coping skills in journalism school. I remember Ross telling a much younger me, journalism is not a self-contemplative body of people. We don't, as a group, often stop to think about the job—in part because many of us are too busy just trying to make deadlines. But as we start to understand that covering trauma requires us to deal with trauma's impact on our lives, it's time to have that conversation.

Making sure people see their reflection in the mirror has never been more important. Breaking through the noise to deliver the news is now our most critical function—but so is taking care of ourselves.

I hope the lessons on the pages that follow help start that process because we need journalists now more than ever.

PREFACE

Giving Up a Little Bit of Your Soul

"If you are a good journalist, what you do is live a lot of things vicariously and report them for other people who want to live vicariously."

—*Harry Reasoner*

I believe that telling stories for a living, being a journalist, is important, exciting, terrifying, frustrating, eye opening, and maybe the most fun you can have at work. But it is also a job that changes your soul, one drip at a time.

I had a wise mentor tell me early in my broadcast news career that "every time you are on TV telling a story you must give up another bit of your soul". He was right. It's like a water faucet dripping on the ground. If it drips long enough, you will have another Grand Canyon! I have seen victories and tragedies. I have witnessed unspeakable physical trauma. I have been terrified and angry, cold and wet, tired and excited, hired and fired. When a doctor is trying to stop the bleeding on a patient, they don't think about the blood. They think about the job.

That's what I did, but my soul was paying attention the entire time. Even good stories, the happy stories, or the success stories can slowly and quietly change who you are. Remember, change isn't always bad. Maybe your soul needs changing.

During my 50 years chasing news stories, my soul went through a lot. Each story I covered changed me in some way. I didn't know it at the time, but each one taught me something about myself or the world around me. Looking back on them is bringing back the lessons that changed my soul. I would not trade my experiences for a predictable office job. I loved what I did. I craved it.

If you are a journalist, you will have your own journey. Give your soul a glass of bourbon and get it ready for a rough but rewarding ride. If you are NOT a public storyteller, then this book and my journey might help you figure out how to watch the news or to deal with the challenges in your life. Each story contains a simple truth. It may be honesty or compassion. It may be risk or anger. Each story teaches a lesson about life and its fragility or wonder.

My journalism career began in high school writing for the *Preble Buzz* school newspaper. While in college I interned at WLUK-TV in Green Bay, and when I graduated from college, I went to work at WFRV-TV, also in my hometown. After 3 years, I moved to WTHR in Indianapolis. This is where I really grew as a reporter. Three more years and the phone rang at my desk. It was Johnathon Rodgers, the news director at KNXT-TV in Los Angeles (later, KCBS). I spent a decade there, and in 1990 I was hired as the main anchor at Very Independent KCOP-TV in L.A. You will read stories in this book from all these stations. Five years later, in 1995, my family and I left Los Angeles for Kentucky. We formed a company and bought a series of local radio stations. Our plan was to run them and then sell them. Five years later we did sell them, and I went to work as a reporter and anchor for MSNBC in New York. This was just after 9/11, and it was very somber working so close to ground zero. After about a year of reporting and anchoring for the national cable outlet, I was hired by KNTV in Las Vegas as the main anchor. When Journal Broadcasting went from a private company to a publicly held entity, things changed, and my anchor salary was more than the general manager could take. He refused to renew my contract after 3 years. So I went back to southern California and worked for KNBC in Los Angeles as a reporter and anchor.

Ok, I know it seems as if I can't hold a job, but this is how the business goes sometimes. My time at KNBC also came to an end due to budget cuts and I was off to anchor the news at KTVX in Salt Lake City. Three years later, the station was sold, and the new owners cut the budgets and let some of the staff go. You guessed it—I was on the list. This time I headed back south to San Diego and KUSI-TV, where I was a reporter and anchored the 11 pm newscast. The next career choice was mine.

After 7 years in San Diego, I was hired as news director at KMIR-TV in Palm Desert, California. About a year into my tenure, the station was sold, and the position of news director was cut. The anchor became the newsroom leader. I was out the door again. This time I went back to the Midwest. I became the main anchor at KAAL-TV in Rochester, Minnesota, working for the same news director who fired me in Las Vegas. It's a strange business. Two years later, it was time to retire from work on the air. Along with two colleagues, I started a coaching and a training company called Top News Talent (www.topnewstalent.com). I also have a mentoring website, www.tvnewsmentor.com

That is my journey. Thank you for sharing my career with me. I hope you find something in each one of these stories, just like I did.

ANCHORING THE NEWS AT KUSI TV IN SAN DIEGO

MY FIRST "REAL" JOB IN BROADCAST JOURNALISM

"Life is a tiger you have to grab by the tail, and if you don't know the nature of the beast it will eat you up."

—*Stephen King*

I was a student at the University of Wisconsin–Platteville and home for the summer. I needed a job and I had just been named news director of the college radio station. The internship in the news department at WAPL in Appleton was posted on the college internship job board. I jumped at it. And that is how I started my professional career in broadcast journalism.

Appleton is about 25 miles from Green Bay, so if I was going to do this, I would have to drive every weekday to work. My parents worked with me figuring out gas money and food, so I could still make some money for the savings account before I returned to classes as a sophomore in the fall.

WAPL hired me. I think it was probably $3 an hour. I was going to be the only news person at the station, and I would work the morning shift, from 5 am to noon. The job meant finding the news, writing the news, and then going on the air twice an hour with a newscast. I was stoked. I had been bitten by the broadcast journalism bug and this was going to be a fantastic summer. On my first day, I began learning about the reality of broadcasting and not just the fantasy. They told me I should use the name "Ross Roberts" on the air.

The station played country music and went on the air every morning at six. The morning DJ was a radio veteran. Jack Watson had jumped around at many stations in the area for years but had finally settled in at WAPL. He was rough around the edges and usually came in with alcohol on his breath. On my first day, I stopped at the Outagamie County Sheriff's Office desk and the Appleton Police Department dispatch center on my way into the station. I would get copies of the incident and arrest reports overnight. These had a treasure trove of local news, but you had to interpret them and do follow-up calls. I usually arrived at the "cop shops" about 4:30 in the morning. I would then have enough time to go through the reports, get to the station, and write the first newscast of that morning.

Day one went great. I was excited and exhausted. I didn't make any major mistakes. Jack came in and signed on the station. He made sure I knew the ropes and I got the news on the air. I went home that day feeling like my career was already starting to take shape. I began settling in.

Day two, same thing. Same with day three. But on Thursday morning of my first week at work, I was tested.

The radio station was on the top floor of a 10-story office building in downtown Appleton. I had to park and take an old elevator up 10 floors. I was usually the first one there, so I unlocked the door and went right to the newsroom to begin writing and preparing. Sometimes I was so focused I never even heard Jack coming off the elevator and heading to the main studio to begin his shift. He had to turn on the transmitter and get the first song ready for the day. But on this first

Thursday of my first real broadcasting job, I was "thrown to the wolves". I was scrambling to finish my 6 am newscast. When I was done it was 5:55 and I grabbed my stack of news stories and headed for the studio. I pushed open the door and no Jack! We were 4 minutes from going on the air and I was alone in the studio!

My experience from the college radio station kicked in. I knew how to fire up the transmitter and I knew I had to play the opening announcement required by the FCC. But, I thought, *What will I do if Jack doesn't show up?* I flipped all the switches, I played the "cart" with the recorded announcements, and I cued up a record. As soon as the announcement played, I cracked open the microphone and began my morning newscast. It was supposed to last 5 minutes. All along I had one eye on the studio door, hoping Jack Watson would appear. He did, with 1 minute to spare. He came in with very sleepy eyes and a sly smile on his face. I was still reading my newscast on the air when he plopped in the main studio chair, yawned, and took a deep breath. I ended the newscast with "and now here's the Fox Valley's Country Giant morning man, Jack Watson!" His voice boomed out "Good Morning" over the microphone and he flipped the switch for the first song that I had cued for him. Buck Owens' "I've Got a Tiger by the Tail" came screaming out the studio speakers. We were on the air, and I had survived my first crisis.

Jack's late arrival became a habit. He knew I could do it, so he began cutting it closer and closer and every day I would get WAPL Radio on the air. One morning Jack came to me in the newsroom after his shift was done at about 10 o'clock. He said, "Hey, Ross, thanks for covering my ass in the morning when I am late, but could you pick another song for Christ's sake?" You see, every day that he was late I cued up the same song to start his show. I hoped he would get tired of it and maybe make it in to work earlier. He never did. I really did have a tiger by the tail.

In the fall, I went back to classes and left WAPL behind. I will never forget how working there made me feel.

ONE MOMENT IN TIME

"I am in the right place, at the right time, doing the right thing."

—*Louise L. Hay*

When I came to work this December morning in 1976, I had no idea I was about to deliver some news that would make a man collapse in tears into my arms.

It was cold but clear when I walked to the car in the TV station parking lot. We packed our gear into the brightly colored Chevy painted with the letters WFRV 5-Country Eyewitness News. The photographer and I had a two-hour drive ahead of us. I had argued against doing this story at the morning meeting because it had happened overnight, and by the time we would get from the studio in Green Bay to Peshtigo, Wisconsin, there would be no story left to get. But we were told to go, and we did.

It was just a short five sentences we ripped off the Associated Press wire. It said, "Three people died in a house fire overnight. A mother and her two children were killed when the fire spread quickly. Firefighters worked in the cold to put out the blaze. The preliminary cause blamed the husband for overfilling a wood stove. One firefighter was injured." I called the fire department before heading out on the road. The dispatcher said they were still mopping up at the scene.

It was about noon when we arrived on the outskirts of Peshtigo. It was my first time there, but it was a famous place to people from Wisconsin. We had all heard about the great Peshtigo fire in our history classes. In 1871, on the same night as the great Chicago fire, a huge forest fire consumed the entire town. Twelve hundred people had died in the Peshtigo fire. There were over three million acres burned. There's a museum there with all the details. It is still the largest wildfire in U.S. history. Other than that, Peshtigo is just another beautiful little Wisconsin town. Now, another fire there would affect my life.

We had the address of this overnight house fire, and it was about two miles out of town on a two-lane country road. It was farm country, but on this day the ground was all white. The snow was thick on the fields, and you could only see about half of the old wooden fence posts holding up rusted barbed wire.

We rounded a corner and saw the house. The white two-bedroom place was still standing . . . but most of the roof was gone and the white snow around it was covered with black soot and cracked pieces of wood and charred insulation that firefighters had ripped away during the firefight.

The driveway was short and rutted and it led to the side of the house and a small garage out back. As we pulled in, we saw two fire trucks parked next to the garage. Several men were still pulling hoses into one of the trucks.

My photographer began filming the scene and I walked up the slippery rear concrete steps of the burned-out house. I entered through the kitchen. The ceiling had collapsed, and this tiny space was filled with charred wood and ceiling tiles. On the counter were the things that said "family". I saw a cookie jar with a bear painted on the front. I saw mixing bowls and coffee cups.

I stepped over the debris and walked into a hallway leading to the front of the house. As I got to the living room, I stopped dead. It was hard to tell it was a Christmas tree. The fire made it look like black wrought iron and underneath it, surprisingly not burned, were toys and other remnants of a happy Christmas morning. Just 24 hours ago this family had shared a warm, loving holiday in this room. Now, the room was gone, and most of the family was gone too. I just stood there. Across the room, I saw the wood stove that the firefighters said was overfilled and probably caused this family tragedy.

We did the interview with the fire chief and were getting ready to leave when an official-looking car pulled up. It was the local fire marshal to inspect the place and confirm the cause. We hung around and found out that the preliminary cause—the overfilled stove was not the cause at all. Turns out, according to the fire marshal, it was an accident. A wire stapled into the wooden rafters in the basement had shorted out and the heat ignited some old insulation.

We headed into town for a sandwich, but something told me this story was not over. After eating at the local café, I said to the photographer, "Let's make one more stop at the house before heading back to Green Bay."

We drove into the driveway and noticed the fire trucks were gone. There was just one car parked in the back. As I walked toward the house, a man in a white T-shirt and black jeans walked toward me down the steps. His eyes met mine. He had one arm in a sling and his face was covered with soot. My first thought was that this was the injured firefighter who had come back this morning to see the place.

The man took one step down and then sat down on those cold concrete steps. I walked up next to him and simply said, "Hi!" His eyes rose up and they filled with tears.

He said, "I killed them." My heart stopped. This man sitting here in front of me was the husband and the father of the three people who died just a few feet away in his burned-out house. "I killed them", he repeated. "I filled that stove too full, and I killed my own family."

I found myself sitting next to him as he cried. My photographer had grabbed the camera and was standing about 15 feet away. He laid the microphone down nearby.

The husband and father just kept repeating, "I killed them, I can't go on." I wanted to tell him that he had not killed them, and that it was an accident of just a faulty wire. Then I realized he didn't know that. He had not met the fire marshal. He still thought it was his fault!

I grabbed his hand. I don't know why, I said, "Listen to me, I am a reporter, and I was here when the fire marshal found that it was not the overfilled stove. It was a short in a wire in the basement. It was an accident; it wasn't you!" I heard my own voice. It sounded as if I was pleading for him to stop hurting. I wanted him to know. I wanted to help take away the pain.

He looked at me and said, "What?"

I repeated the fire marshal's story. The man started sobbing uncontrollably. He collapsed into my arms. I will never forget what he said to me: "I thought I had killed my family, and I knew I could not live with that on my heart. I don't know how I can live without my kids and my wife, but knowing I didn't kill them gives me something to hang on to. I was ready to just kill myself right here, right now."

I told him, again, it was not his fault and he just cried. We sat there for about 15 minutes, not saying a word. Then he got up and looked back toward the door of the house where his loving wife and children had died. Then, he looked at me and said, "Thank you." He shuffled to his car and drove off.

Our drive back to Green Bay that day was very quiet. When I aired my story that night, we used the video of my encounter with this man, and I shared my experience with the viewers.

It was "my" Peshtigo fire. Not the one history records in that museum, the one that killed hundreds of people back in the 1800s, but a small fire one day after Christmas in 1976 that I will never forget. Even as a reporter you can't forget you are still a person. And, sometimes, you are part of the story.

THE BLUE-EYED TRAITOR

"Those who hate you don't win unless you hate them, and then you destroy yourself."

—*Louis C. K.*

According to one of the people I interviewed for a major investigation I did, I am a "blue-eyed traitor". It was an accusation that led to the end of an interview session and a very tense, potentially dangerous next few hours.

I first interviewed the grand dragon of the California Ku Klux Klan in the early 1980s. That interview led to the realization that a new group was forming, disguised as a pseudo religion. I was a reporter at KCBS in Los Angeles and we set out to expose the group and its potentially dangerous tactics and methods.

The so-called Aryan Nation Church of Jesus Christ Christian was headquartered in Sandpoint, Idaho, and was led by a man claiming to be a minister. Pastor Richard Butler set up a camp in the wilderness where followers could come for rifle target practice and meetings that were more like racist pep rallies. Their ranks were growing and branching out to states all over the west, including California.

I went to Idaho along with a photographer and a producer. We checked into the Holiday Inn on the shores of Hayden Lake. We did not have an interview scheduled. The plan was to drive to the camp and talk our way in. The dirt road into the Aryan Nation camp was protected by a guard house and a gate. Standing next to the small shack was a guard carrying a semi-automatic rifle. A sign on the front of the gate said, "No Jews Allowed". It was clear this was not a friendly bunch. After a few minutes and some calls back and forth to the camp headquarters, we were turned away. We would not be allowed in. However, Pastor Butler agreed to meet with us and answer questions the next day in a room at the nearby Holiday Inn.

I had done plenty of confrontational interviews before, but this one would be different. We were on their turf and didn't know if those around us at the hotel were part of the group. We kept a low profile in town that evening.

The next morning at breakfast it became clear we were being watched. We noticed several people in the hotel restaurant who were clearly there to keep an eye on us. About 10 o'clock we got the call. Pastor Butler would meet us in room 1425.

After lunch we took the elevator to the 14th floor. We had our camera gear and the notes and research we had worked on outlining the hateful and racist publications and teachings of the Aryan Nation group. We wanted to find out just how dangerous this new group could become.

I am White. My producer was White, and the photographer was White. According to the group's teachings, of course, we were not the "enemy". We were greeted by Pastor Butler. He looked like a grandfather. He was in his 60s with white hair, wearing a dark suit. He handed me his card. It had the Aryan Nation symbol on it. He asked how we had heard about his group and why we were interested. I told him about my interviews with the Klan leader in Los Angeles and talked about the gang problem in the big cities of the west. It was benign conversation while our photographer set up his gear.

The interview began. We talked about the organization and Butler told us why he started the Aryan Nation church, as he called it. After about 10 minutes of general philosophy, I wanted to get to the meat of his philosophy. It was a hate group, but Butler claimed it was simply an organization to promote the ideals of White Americans.

I pulled out one of the flyers we had found posted on a telephone pole in the small community of Hayden Lake. It was clearly posted there to terrorize. It showed pictures of Black people depicted as monkeys. It showed caricatures of men with big noses with the words "kill the mongrel Jews". It showed other pictures of Asians with their eyes exaggerated. One of the flyers headlines said, "Don't let these animals invade our town".

I looked at him and held up the flyer. Pointing to it, I said, "Pastor Butler, why do you hate Blacks?" He said he didn't hate them. I asked, "Why do you hate Jews?" He said he didn't, despite my showing him a flyer that indicated otherwise. So, I said, "Why do you hate Asians?"

Again, he said, "I don't hate Asians."

He was clearly getting agitated. Finally, I said, "Well, I am looking at this flyer and it's clear that you do. So, if you don't hate Blacks, Jews, or Asians, who do you hate?"

There was a long pause. The armed men standing just outside of camera range began to inch toward Butler. I didn't know if I had crossed a line. Butler leaned forward and said, "Who do I hate? I hate blue-eyed traitors like you. This interview is over."

He stood up. The armed guards walked him to the door, and he was gone. We were left in the room at the hotel with two other men with guns. Clearly, they were not happy about the way this had ended. They told us to pack up, now.

The ride down in the elevator was tense. The two men led us to the lobby and warned us to stay away from the camp. We were now the enemy of the Aryan Nation. I was the blue-eyed traitor. It would not be the end of my confrontations with members of this group.

We found out that day that racism has no color. It's more about being an enemy, and we became the enemy to a group of dangerous people. Butler had to know I was going to ask those questions. Turns out he didn't really have to answer them. His actions spoke much louder.

(We found out about a year later that one of the armed men guarding Pastor Butler that day was later convicted of murdering Denver radio talk show host Alan Berg.)

GOP CONVENTION 1980, DETROIT

A VERY CLOSE CALL

"I'm sure there are close calls that we're not even aware of hundreds of times a year. You cross the street, and if you'd crossed the street two minutes later, you'd have been hit by a car, but you'd never know it."

—Seth MacFarlane

Most of the time we were rushing to stories, but this time the story came rushing to us, with the velocity of a speeding bullet.

It was a rainy, cold fall day in Indianapolis in 1979, and I had worked all day. It was 7 o'clock and I returned home to my small studio apartment on the north side when my pager went off. As I grabbed a Coke from the refrigerator, I also grabbed the phone and called the assignment desk. They needed me to check out some police action developing in my neighborhood.

The photographer arrived at my apartment door a few minutes later in the Ford Bronco loaded down with equipment, and we headed east just a few blocks to an apartment complex. The on-and-off rain of the day was now a cold downpour. You could hear the raindrops on the leaves of the trees surrounding the building.

When we pulled into the complex, the place was crawling with police. We were blocked from the main parking lot, but an officer told us the command post was set up around the south side of the building.

I walked over to the man in charge, and he told me that a team of officers had tried to serve a warrant on a man in one of the apartments. This man was mentally unstable, he said, and the warrant was an authorization to take him in for treatment. But, instead of cooperating, the man had pushed the officers away, locked the apartment door, and was threatening to shoot them. The cops believed he had several guns.

So far, they established phone contact with him, and the SWAT team was called to stand by. This was a standoff, but clearly the police were not interested in using force to take in a mental patient. I called the assignment desk on the radio and told them the story. The night desk suggested I just stay there and see what happens. It was going to be a long night.

We were with the cops in the parking lot, but we could not see the actual apartment, and we knew if we were going to get any video to help tell the story, we had to find a spot where we could see the action. This was the right thing to do, but it turned out to be a very dangerous thing to do.

It was now getting late, and the rain was not letting up. The police were hunkering down for a long night of trying to negotiate with a crazy man to get him to lay down his guns and come out. We drove our news van into a school parking lot next to the apartment complex, where we could see the double-glass patio doors and the kitchen window of the apartment where the man was holed up. There was a small grove of trees between the building and us but the trees were sparse, and we kept moving closer and closer to get a better look.

We got to a point where we were no more than 50 yards from that double-glass door. We parked the truck and waited. I was in the driver's seat. My photographer was in the passenger seat, holding the camera so he could be ready if anything happened.

We could see the SWAT team in place on either side of the apartment. They were waiting, too. Inside the apartment, I could occasionally see the shadow of the man moving around. We waited and waited and waited for hours and the rain kept falling.

Then, suddenly, I heard a crash! I stood up next to the open driver's-side door and my photographer did the same on his side of the truck. He lifted the camera to his shoulder and I grabbed the microphone and held it above my head while standing behind the truck door.

The SWAT team had lobbed a tear gas canister into the apartment. I could see the gas billowing in the kitchen and the police with guns drawn beginning to move closer to those double-glass patio doors. We had a great view of the action. The police were making their move and we were going to get it all on videotape. The tear gas worked, but it turned out our efforts to get the best pictures also put us directly in the line of fire.

I was standing behind the driver's door, and I saw the double-glass patio door slide open. Out of the cloud of tear gas, I saw the man. He was coming out. He had a gun in each hand and they were pointed right at us. The police were yelling; I could not make out what they were saying. The camera was rolling, and the microphone was ready.

The man did not drop the guns; he started firing. The first bullet hit the front of our truck with a "ping", but I really didn't realize it was a bullet. I was focused on the man. Then the next bullets hit the grill, "ping, ping". He kept shooting. My head was in the "V" formed by the truck door and the frame, and I felt it brush my ear. A bullet had missed my head by less than an inch. I felt it whiz by! I dove into the driver's seat and the photographer jumped in on the passenger side. "Ping, ping, ping". Three more slugs hit the front of the truck. My photographer lifted the camera back up again, pointing it toward the apartment.

The man had stumbled on the lawn and the police had him in their sights. "Boom! Boom!" The guns went off! The man fell immediately. The standoff was over.

I looked at my photographer and I could see from the look on his face that he felt the same as I did. All I said was "I guess we got too close." And he said, "I guess so."

We were nearly killed. One headlight on the truck had been shattered. It was a very close call, but that fact became even more dramatic when we returned to the TV station early that morning and put the videotape into the playback machine.

The photographer had gotten it all! We had the billowing tear gas and the SWAT team ready to pounce. We had the patio door flying open and the man with the guns staggering outside. And, we had the bullets. When the tape got to the point where the slug came close to me, it was the sound that shocked me. I was holding the microphone about two inches from my head while standing next to the truck. When I played the videotape, you could hear the bullet go past it, and it was a sound I will never forget. That bullet went screaming past that microphone with a "zzzeeeeeeeeeeeaaaaaammmmmmmmmmm"! I could actually hear how close I came to dying. I will never forget the sound of my very close call. Life is fragile.

RIDE, SALLY RIDE

"With courage you will dare to take risks, have the strength to be compassionate, and the wisdom to be humble. Courage is the foundation of integrity."

—*Keshavan Nair*

I was lucky enough during my career to interview some real heroes. One of them didn't think of herself as one. That is what I remember most about my time with Sally Ride.

Astronaut Sally Ride was one of the first women in the U.S. space program and ended up being the first woman in space for the United States. It was May of 1983 when KCBS sent me to Houston to talk with her about her upcoming historic mission.

Sally Ride was from Encino, California, so she was a local girl whose family still lived in the San Fernando Valley, right in the middle of our viewing area. I was excited to meet her. She had been training for years and was about one month away from climbing into the *Challenger* Space Shuttle as a mission specialist for STS-7, as it was called.

We met in a huge hangar at the Houston Space Center complex. She was still training every day and the hangar was filled with mock-ups of the shuttle payload bay and command center. She would move from one to the other learning all the jobs on board, just in case.

We shook hands and said hello. She looked like a teenager with big, puffy hair and a wide smile. I was expecting to talk with a "hero"; instead, I got Sally. She was one of a kind. Almost embarrassed by her celebrity status.

"Do we have to do this?" she said with a smile. She told me she just wanted to be a scientist and engineer and do it in space. She said she was not used to all this attention. We talked. I interviewed her and asked all the right questions, and she gave all the right answers. She represented NASA well and she was an inspiration to girls who dreamed of following in her footsteps.

I am always amazed by the people I meet who I think will be different. Sally Ride was confident but almost apologetic. She told me she really didn't like all the publicity, but understood it came with the territory. She was a smiling, down-to-earth person who was getting ready to leave Earth and represent women in space. For her it was important that she was seen as a professional and not just a woman. It was also important, she said, that girls realized they could do anything, not just fly in space.

So why is this important to us? It is the first time I learned that you could be confident and humble, scared and determined. I saw all of that in Sally Ride. I also felt the tremendous weight on her shoulders. Women around the world were watching. They wanted Sally to succeed and carry their spirits into space with them.

It would have been easy for Sally Ride, from Encino, California, to have her head swell so it would not fit into that space helmet. Hers did not swell. Her heart did. She told me how rewarding it was to know so many young girls were looking up to her. She told me she just wanted to "not screw up", and she said it with that big Sally Ride smile.

She was confident and humble and scared and determined. I thought to myself, *What a great way to be.*

I INTERVIEWED O. J. AND NO ONE SAW IT!

(Except Geraldo)

"The day you take complete responsibility for yourself, the day you stop making any excuses, that's the day you start to the top."

—*O. J. Simpson*

In January of 1996, a producer named Tony Hoffman hired me to conduct a 90-minute interview with O. J. Simpson. It was the first and only interview granted after his acquittal on murder charges. The plan was to include the interview on a videotape that would be marketed directly to news consumers, so they could see and hear O. J. tell the story of what happened the night his wife was killed along with her friend Ron Goldman.

The plan never worked quite like the producer had planned.

From the day I received the phone call offering me the opportunity, to the wild and secretive trip to the Rockingham mansion to conduct the interview, to the days following word that O. J. had talked to me, to the fallout following the release of the video, this is a story filled with drama and conflict and insight into the world of journalism, tabloid TV, small-town politics, and petty jealousy.

OH, yes, Geraldo was angry. He called me and told me that I was a punk and a sellout. He was angry that I had got the interview, and he hadn't. In the end, the *National Enquirer* refused the advertisement to sell the tape. The producer sued NBC News. Most of the tapes were never sold and may still be in a warehouse.

So, I interviewed O. J. and "virtually" no one saw it. But the lessons learned and the choices made during the negotiations to do the interview are compelling and fascinating.

The phone call came during the first holiday party I was throwing for my new radio station staff in Elizabethtown, Kentucky. It was Tony Hoffman telling me about this plan to have me interview O. J. Simpson and the interview would be distributed and sold to the public on a VHS tape.

My lawyer, George Bane, and I spent about a week negotiating a deal. The money part was easy. The hardest part was negotiating the requirements to preserve the journalistic integrity of the interview. I insisted on several "rules" that would guarantee that the interview would be included on the tape as it was recorded with no editing.

I lived in Elizabethtown, a town of about 25,000 people in north central Kentucky, and I was a new local business owner. The acquittal of O. J. was a big story here, just as it was in most places worldwide. There I was making plans to do an interview with him while at the same time trying to keep it a secret from those in town and my own radio station news director.

I quietly left town heading for Los Angeles. When I arrived at the airport, I was picked up by a woman assigned to me as a researcher. We drove to the Holiday Inn along the San Diego freeway at Sunset Blvd and checked in. There were rumors that I was in town and that I was going to interview O. J. The producers had security in the lobby.

I was in the room, going over thousands of pages of courtroom testimony, finalizing my list of questions, and looking for things that might help me show another side of the man who never took the witness stand. The phone rang. I picked it up. It was a reporter from a local TV station who I had worked with. She found me. The fact that I was in Los Angeles after moving to Kentucky was a clear sign that something was up.

The stories on the 11 pm news in Los Angeles that night were about me and O. J. and the secret interview.

In the morning. I met a lawyer hired by Tony Hoffman to assist me with the interview. We met in my hotel room, and I began to discuss the case. He seemed cold, distant, and frankly, scared. When the time came to go, we headed to the hotel lobby and were hustled by security into a van. There were TV cameras there and reporters were yelling questions. The van had its windows covered with dark paper. We sat in silence all the way to the Rockingham mansion and through the gates, again guarded by photographers and reporters. We were inside, but the carnival was just beginning.

It was a mad house inside O. J's Rockingham mansion. The production crew was setting up lights and cameras, so I was ushered into a formal living room, and along with my lawyer I sat down to go over the rules. Producer and photographer Larry Schiller was there and so were some people from *People* magazine I had never met. This was the first time I discovered that *People* had purchased the picture and story rights on the day of the interview.

I went through the ground rules I had established for my part of the interview. I had all my information and questions in my laptop computer, and neither O. J. nor anyone from the production team had seen them. I had total control of the content. I would be alone with O.

J. in the room, except for the two photographers. Down the hallway, in Kato Kaelin's room, there was a production area where my attorney was to sit and monitor the production. The producers agreed to shoot and distribute the interview just as I had recorded it. When it was over, my attorney was to receive a complete copy of the 90-minute interview with timecode. The deal was that if anything was edited or changed when the final tape was released, I would blow the whistle on the entire project. I wanted journalistic integrity, and I got it.

It was time to talk to O. J. The interview flew by. I remember very little of my thoughts or impressions during the time I was face-to-face with O. J. other than thinking how "cool" and calm he seemed. That was until I began talking about race and its role in the "not guilty" verdict. Then, he seemed to tense up and get angry at any suggestion that he was acquitted because the jury was primarily Black. I asked him repeatedly, "Did you kill your wife?" He said no.

After the interview O. J. disappeared. I was asked by one of the members of the production crew if I would like a tour of the house. He showed me Kato's room and where the police said they had found blood spots in the front entry and on the driveway, and then he led me down the narrow gravel walkway next to the garage where police said they had found the bloody glove. My impression was there was no way O. J. could have fought through the snarled bushes and climbed that 6-foot-high fence as the police had alleged.

I flew back to Louisville immediately after the shoot. The deal included my silence about the interview and its contents until after the formal release of the videotape for sale in about two weeks. But that was not going to last. At my tiny radio station in Elizabethtown, the phone was already ringing. The pressure was on. I interviewed O. J., and the world wanted to know what he said and why I did it and how

I got the interview and they didn't. The angriest person, it seemed, was Geraldo Rivera.

We got hundreds of calls at our radio stations for interview requests. Everyone from Sally Jessy Raphael to Jenny Jones (who sent a new live potted plant every day) to *Inside Edition* to *A Current Affair*. They all wanted to interview me for their shows.

I did some local interviews and I appeared "live" on *Good Morning America*.

Everyone wanted to know if O. J. confessed. I had the freedom to say what he did "not" say, so I told everyone he did not confess, but I was prevented from telling them what he did say about the killing, the glove, the blood, etc.

Geraldo Rivera called me, and I had a 30-minute conversation with him. He wanted to know how I could put money in the pocket of a killer. I told him that O. J. was acquitted and that if he was making any money on this project, I was not aware of it. I was hired to ask him the tough questions and I did it.

After a few days of negotiating with the tape producer, Tony Hoffman made a deal with *Dateline* NBC to do a story about the production of the tape, and I agreed to an interview with Chris Larsen. He and his crew came to Elizabethtown and conducted the interview in the office of the radio station. He kept asking me how much O. J. was getting for the interview. I kept telling him that I did not know and to me it did not matter as long as the interview I conducted was journalistically sound. It was.

When the videotape went on sale about 4 weeks after the interview, the *National Enquirer* refused to take advertisements for the tape, calling the project "tawdry". Tony Hoffman, the producer, was already in a battle with NBC. He claimed *Dateline* agreed to air the 800 number to buy the tape when they used excerpts during the story. They did not use the number, so Tony was suing them (he eventually lost).

We simply attempted to get back to normal in our small-town radio station. However, for months the rumors swirled in Elizabethtown that O. J. Simpson was a financial partner in our radio stations. The owner of a competing station had started the vicious rumor.

Tony Hoffman told me he sold about 8,000 videotapes. He had hoped to sell half a million. The last I heard, they were still in boxes in a warehouse in Westlake Village, California. I have one of them I purchased on eBay. I also have a tape "sleeve", signed by O. J. To this day I don't know if O. J. ever got any money. I suspect he agreed to give all tape proceeds to Robert Kardashian to pay for legal expenses. He was a partner in the project with Tony Hoffman.

My interview with O. J. stands as the only interview he conducted during the period between the criminal and civil trials. It was journalistically sound and was the only time he answered in his own words the questions raised at the trial.

I am always asked if I think he did it. "What do you think, Ross?" Well, I have an opinion, but if you watch the video and see how he answers the questions, you can look into his eyes and decide for yourself. It's the only video record we have that will give us that insight. I am proud of it.

THE ENERGY OF A MONSTER

"Man is the cruelest animal."

—*Friedrich Nietzsche*

T here are times when you can just "feel" the energy of a monster in the room. It happened to me in a Salt Lake City courtroom in 2009 when I was sent by ABC 4 KTVX, to tell the story of Elizabeth Smart.

Her nine-month physical ordeal was over. She had been kidnapped by a man from her bedroom when she was just 14 years old and was now ready to tell her story on the witness stand. The entire world would know the sexual brutality that she endured.

Brian David Mitchell was on trial, accused of the kidnapping. When they led him into that courtroom and sat him down, his hands and feet were shackled. You could hear the chains. But you could hear him too. First, wheezing, breathing heavily as he sat in the oak courtroom chair. Elizabeth was not in the room yet and at this hearing, they would never be face-to-face in court.

Mitchell started singing church hymns. The words were barely understandable, gibberish mostly, and the judge asked him to stop. He kept on singing. He had long hair and a beard, and he just kept singing despite repeated warnings from the bench. You could feel the anger and you could hear it in his voice. Finally, the judge reached his limit. He ordered Mitchell out of the courtroom. The monster was gone, for now. He would not hear the testimony from his victim.

Then Smart walked in, wearing a white blouse and black pants and her blonde hair pulled back. Stoic, calm, and focused, she raised her hand to take the oath and began to tell the story of what the "monster" did to her. She didn't cry. She just poured out the horrible tale. "He performed a ceremony to marry me to him and after that he proceeded to rape me," she said. It took her two hours to tell the whole story of how she was raped every day, sometimes three or four times, while Mitchell held her captive.

The prosecutor asked her to describe her kidnapper in a few words. She said, "Evil, wicked, manipulative, sneaky, selfish, greedy, not spiritual, not religious, and not close to God."

Eventually, Mitchell and his girlfriend were both convicted.

It was the contrast that strikes me to this day. The determined calmness of Elizabeth Smart to tell the world how this monster had treated her and the crazy antics of the man who had treated her like an animal.

In that courtroom on that day, we could all feel the energy of a monster.

ON THE NEWS DESK AT ABC 4 IN SALT LAKE CITY. PHOTO BY AMBER SIGMAN

JELLY ON A SPOON

"Life is short, and it is up to you to make it sweet."

—*Jean-Jacques Rousseau*

When I coach young journalists, I tell them a story about my grandma. What she did with jelly on a spoon can help them with their storytelling, and it can help anyone facing a complicated set of facts they need to communicate.

As a boy I would spend part of my summer vacations at my grandparents' cottage on Chain Lake in northern Wisconsin. It was an idyllic time. Our days were filled with fishing and gardening and swimming in the lake. Sometimes I would spend up to a month there during the summer and sometimes I would get sick. Nothing serious, just a headache or the flu or maybe a slight fever. That's when Grandma brought out the jelly-filled spoon.

I had a hard time swallowing pills, especially aspirin. To me it was chalky and had hard edges and I always gagged. So, Grandma came up with a solution. She would crush the two aspirin tablets in a big spoon and then put a quarter-size dollop of grape jelly right on top of the powder. She would stir it a bit, and then it was easy for me to swallow. I got the medicine I needed because it was surrounded by something yummy.

As a journalist and a storyteller, we are constantly confronted with complicated but critical information that needs to be communicated to our viewers and readers, but how do you do that without them "gagging" on the rough edges? It's all about combining journalism with storytelling, and one cannot exist without the other.

Finding the right interview to help put the facts into perspective, finding the human angle to a story, or finding the interesting video or sound to draw the viewer or listener into the story will help make sure they hear and understand the critical information. All of this is the "jelly" to make the medicine go down easily.

My grandmother knew I needed the aspirin to feel better. Instead of making it a bad thing, she found a way to make it enjoyable. If you do the same with information, your journalism will become more powerful. Thanks, Grandma. I still love grape jelly.

MUD AND FIRE AND DEATH

"Life changes fast. Life changes in the instant. You sit down to dinner and life as you know it ends."

—*Joan Didion*

I walked into the KCBS newsroom this Friday morning dressed, as usual, in my suit and tie, ready to end the week on a high note. I was early that day, August 2, 1985, and the newsroom was nearly empty. I was walking toward my office when the news director Erik Sorenson met me in the hallway. He said, "Hey, Becker, are you ready to go?" I smiled and asked him where to. He asked me to follow him to the assignment desk where the morning crew was already at work and the scanners were cackling.

"There's been a plane crash in Dallas," he said, "and it was headed for Los Angeles. The crew will be ready in a minute or two. Head to the airport, use your company American Express Cards and get yourselves on a plane there."

It was a Delta Flight, 191 and it crashed right at the end of a runway. My head was spinning. This Friday just got very busy and very tense.

Even before we landed in Dallas, it got weird. Seeing a smoking airliner on the ground underneath us as we landed was eerie. We rented a car and headed for the roadblock at the south end of the airport complex. As we went through the gate, the sight of the plane—on the ground, ripped open like a watermelon, still smoldering, charred—was sobering.

Then it started raining again. Federal officials told us it was wind shear that brought the plane down about a mile short of the runway. The pilot flew into a thunderstorm and the strong downdraft in the storm pushed the plane into the ground. According to local police and fire officials, 137 people died and 26 were injured, and the huge chunks of the Lockheed L-1011 sitting there reminded us that they had been alive just a short time ago and ready to land in Dallas for work or a vacation. We began hearing stories from witnesses and first responders about the flight attendants who they found injured or burned when they got to the burning plane. Some of the flight attendants were injured and bleeding and still trying to help those strapped in their seats.

We would end up being there for two days, living in our rental car and the Red Cross tents that were set up. It rained and stormed the entire 48 hours, and my suit was covered with mud. My shoes were destroyed. I remember standing near a fence doing my live reports back to Los Angeles and standing in mud 6 inches deep. It's hard not to complain about your own comfort issues when it's raining, and you are miserable and dirty. But the burned-out hulk of Flight 191 was still there looming over us. Every time I looked at it, I could see the seats, and the luggage scattered in the field, and the charred skin of the jetliner with the word "Delta" partially obscured. People died here and others had their lives changed forever in just a few moments of panic and terror. I was dirty and tired, but I was alive.

When we left Dallas, we took off and flew right over the wreckage. It was another moment to realize that things can change in an instant.

MICKEY AND THE MUSTARD STAIN

"The strangest part about being famous is you don't get to give first impressions anymore. Everyone already has an impression of you before you meet them."

—Kristen Stewart

I don't know why, sometimes, it's the little things that you remember during big moments.

Back in the mid-1980s.

KCBS wanted me to do a series of reports about children in the entertainment business, showcasing the advantages and the pitfalls. We called it, "Twinkle Twinkle Little Star". The list of celebrities was long. Patty Duke, Linda Blair, Shirley Temple-Black, Ron Howard, and many more. All of them were children when they first went to work in Hollywood.

One of the biggest names on the list was Mickey Rooney. Most of you won't know who he was. The actor was a giant movie star, an icon. He began his career in the 1930s, and it lasted 9 decades. His first job was at the age of 4, working for his parents on the vaudeville stage. Rooney died in 2014. But in the 1980s he was still working, and I asked him if I could talk with him about his early career as a child in Hollywood. I had a great partner for this project. Producer Danny Tobias was funny and creative and tenacious. We flew to New York City to meet Rooney at a small theater just off Broadway where he was appearing in a play.

This story does not have any dramatic ending or strange twist. It is just a reminder to you, as it was to me, that the build-up is sometimes bigger than the pay-off.

Danny and I met a freelance photojournalist in New York. He joined us in front of the theater, and we were led inside. The interview with Rooney would take place in his dressing room backstage. The room was the size of a closet. It had a stool and a mirror and an old, torn, and obviously dirty sofa. There was a small clothing rack filled with wrinkled shirts and pants. We were told to set up our camera in here and Mr. Rooney would be in shortly. We were stunned that such an important entertainment icon would allow himself to be interviewed in such a dump! It was dusty and it smelled.

He walked in and it all started to make sense. Major movie and stage star Mickey Rooney plopped himself on the dirty sofa and shook our hands. He was grumpy and curt. He said, "Come on, guys, let's get this over with." We did the interview. I can't remember what he said, but I still remember the stain.

Mickey Rooney was dressed in wrinkled black pants and a green polo shirt. Right in the middle of the shirt, just below the three buttons, there was a huge yellow mustard stain. It is all I could see. I asked him about it. He said, "Yeah, I like hot dogs." That was it.

Afterwards, standing in the pouring rain outside waiting for a taxi, Danny and I looked at each other and just began laughing. It was one of those bizarre moments. That mustard stain is all I can remember about my interview with a major Hollywood legend.

AN OMINOUS NOTE ON THE WINDSHIELD

"Never fire a warning shot. It's a waste of ammunition."

—*Hunter S. Thompson*

In the late 1970s, cocaine was everywhere, even on the streets of Indianapolis, Indiana. As a reporter working for WTHR-TV, I got a tip that led me to the source of some of the illegal drugs, and I found out how desperate those who traffic in the stuff can be.

I was single and I had a group of buddies who together spent a lot of time in the bars and discos of the city during that time. I was also on the air, so many of the people I met knew who I was and what I did. One of those "friends" tipped me off to a story that led me into a potentially dangerous situation.

The tip was that a local car dealership was involved in the movement of cocaine from Florida to Indianapolis. The "friend" said the son of the dealership's owner was the main operator. He would shuttle new cars between dealerships in Florida and Indiana, and in the trunks of those cars he would smuggle large amounts of cocaine. In Indianapolis, he would sell the drugs to local dealers, and they would end up on the streets.

As part of the story, I contacted the Indiana State Police. I was told they were already on the case. Investigators confirmed it but asked me to keep it quiet for a couple of weeks. In the meantime, I was allowed to interview a "witness" they had under protection. It was going to be a big and important story when it finally broke, and I had the exclusive.

Two weeks later the story aired, and the reactions started coming in. The family that owned the dealership was well known in the city. Many viewers had purchased cars there for years and the reactions ran from disbelief to anger with the station for airing the story. The son was officially under investigation, but not yet under arrest. The police had made some arrests of a couple of local dealers who were implicating the son and his father.

We were confident about the story, and I continued doing updates for about a week. We even aired part of the interview I did with the witness who was under police protection. All of this led to a financial hit for the station. The dealership owner called and threatened to cancel all his advertising unless we stopped airing the stories. We refused and the ads were pulled. The station general manager was supportive. It was part of the territory when you were doing important community journalism.

There were personal threats too. Every time the phone rang it seemed it was either someone with another tip about the drug dealing or it was someone criticizing me for attacking a strong local family with an important local business. We knew we were doing something significant. We were just waiting for the state police to make their final move and bust the ring. Of course, my life didn't stop. I went to work and went out with my buddies at night and on the weekend. One night, I wondered if it might be my last and I did something stupid.

On the north side of Indianapolis there was a disco (remember it was the late 1970s) named Lucifers. It was the major gathering place for many young professionals. It was also a place where, if you knew the right people, you could buy cocaine. I was there on a Friday night with my friends. No drugs just alcohol. We were drinking and dancing and having a good time unwinding after another busy week. I was the only reporter.

About midnight we all decided to leave and none of us should have been driving. We were just drunk enough to be dangerous. We all headed to our cars in the disco's parking lot. When I got to my car, I got in and put the key in the ignition. I sat there a moment to, again, decide if driving was a good idea considering our night of drinking. I looked up and saw a note jammed under the windshield wiper of the car.

I got out and grabbed the note. I unfolded it. It was wet. It had been raining. The note said, "Give up the cocaine investigation, or else." Then I read the rest, "Go ahead, start the car. See if the bomb goes off!" I froze.

I sat there for a moment. My head was spinning from the alcohol. My ears were ringing from the hours of listening to booming disco music. I was tired of the phone calls and threats about the cocaine investigation story. I was just doing my job. Bottom line: I was angry. So, I grabbed the key in the ignition and turned it. The car started. There was no explosion. I put the car in gear and drove home. It was a foolish moment. The note was clearly a threat, and I should have called the police and had them check the car, but I was drunk and angry and frustrated. I never told the police or anyone at the station about it.

A few days later the son of the dealer owner was arrested. The state police had a news conference announcing the cocaine ring had been busted. Our stories were accurate and within about a month, the dealership was sold to a new owner who began advertising again on the station.

I think about that moment often. Many investigative reporters are threatened when doing their jobs. Some have even been killed chasing stories. I could have been one of them. I should not have driven that night for two reasons—I was drunk, and I was taking a huge chance by starting that car after finding the note. I was lucky and stupid.

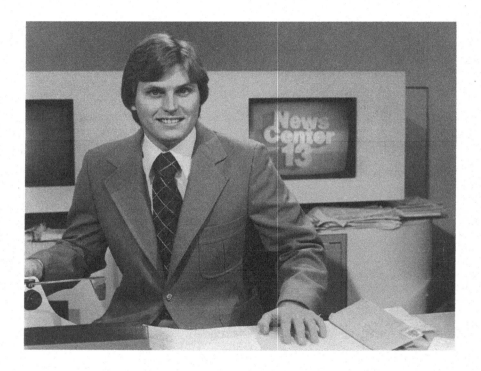

80 MILES AN HOUR IN THE DARK

"Blind risk is stupid, but calculated risks are worth taking."

—*Adam Burch*

I was sleeping. It was 4:30 in the morning and what happened next was not a dream.

My entire house in the San Fernando Valley near Los Angeles began shaking. I held on to the sheets, my eyes wide open in the dark, hoping the roof would not collapse on me, my wife, and my family. It kept shaking and I could hear cracking. I found out later it was the nails popping out of the 2 × 4s that formed our walls and the bathtub swaying back and forth until it cracked the exterior wall. Finally, it stopped. I said to my wife, "Oh, my God, someone is going to die in this one!"

We had lived in southern California for more than 10 years and experienced earthquakes, but this was OUR big one. Just then our bedroom door burst open and our daughter and a foreign exchange student, who was staying with us, ran in crying and jumped in bed with us. They were terrified. We held them and warned them to be ready for aftershocks.

The Northridge earthquake on January 17, 1994, scared the crap out of me. It was the feeling of being so vulnerable. As I lay there listening to the creaking and cracking, there was nothing I could do. I could not run or hide from it. But once the initial shock was over, my reporting instincts started taking over and, stupidly, fear went away. I was very lucky something bad didn't happen to me.

I checked the house. The power was out, but I didn't smell leaking gas. We had a couple of cracked windows, but that's all I could find in the dark. I pulled my wife's car out into the driveway so, if the house collapsed during the aftershocks, she would have a safe place to be. Then, I left. I put on my jeans and grabbed a blue sport coat and kissed them all goodbye with the warning, "I don't know when I will be back." It was my job to be on the air and I was heading into the KCOP newsroom in Hollywood.

It was a weird feeling pulling out of my driveway. With the power out, all the houses and streets were dark. With the car window down, I could still hear the wailing sounds of home and car alarms screaming in the distance. The earthquake had shaken them awake too and there were already aftershocks.

I reached the Ventura Freeway and headed south into the San Fernando Valley. The lanes were deserted. I had KNX NewsRadio on and the anchor was talking about aftershocks and power outages. As I reached Tarzana, I saw the fires burning on either side of the freeway. The smoke was blocking my view. I didn't slow down. I was going 80 miles an hour. I had to get there and the road was clear. It was about a 30-mile drive. I got off the freeway in Hollywood and had to weave around downed and sparking power lines on La Brea Avenue to make it to the KCOP studios.

When I walked into the newsroom, the "live" pictures were flashing on all the monitors showing the collapse of a freeway overpass in Northridge. Cars had plummeted off the ragged ends of the roads and the steel rebar that once helped keep drivers safe was ripped and hanging like snakes escaping from a swamp.

I froze. The images of the damaged freeway were sobering. A California Highway Patrol motorcycle officer was dead after flying off the end of one of those freeways.

I had just driven the Ventura Freeway, in the dark, covered by smoke, at 80 miles an hour and never once even thought that the quake might have damaged the road. It could have happened to me.

We spent the next 24 hours "live" on the air living the aftermath of the quake with the viewers of KCOP. We experienced frightening aftershocks together. We made pleas for blood donations, and we showed people the damage and the rescues. In the few moments I had to think about my own mortality and my family's safety. I thought about my 80-mile-per-hour drive that early morning and how it could have ended in tragedy.

When you are chasing a story, it's exciting. I was focused and determined to do my duty as a journalist. I didn't think about the consequences. I consider that a good thing. It's part of the job.

Maybe I am different.

LIVE REPORTING DURING 1987 EARTHQUAKE IN PASADENA, CA

A BEIGE GREMLIN AND A BIG DECISION ABOUT LIFE

"Love is the absence of judgment."

—*The 14th Dalai Lama*

Working in broadcast journalism is hard on relationships. When my first wife had an affair with a local radio disc jockey just 30 days after we were married, I made a decision that led me to cover stories in Sin City in a beige AMC Gremlin.

Now, why is that important? It's not, but it was a moment in my life, sitting in what could be the ugliest car ever made when I knew what I decided could affect me forever. Moments like that are not forgotten.

The story is simple. I was just out of college and working as a reporter at WFRV-TV in my hometown, Green Bay, Wisconsin. It was September and I had been on the job there for just over 4 months. I took time off in June to get married. When I found out about the affair, I was angry and confused and, I guess, desperate. That desperation led me to start looking for a new job outside of Green Bay to try to save my marriage. I found a job opening at KSHO (now KTNV) in Las Vegas. Reporter and anchor, the ad said, and I applied. I had never been to Las Vegas, but it sounded exciting and just what I needed to springboard my career and take my new wife far away from the "distractions" of Green Bay.

When the Las Vegas station news director called, he said he liked my work and was ready to offer me the position. We talked about money and duties. He said he wanted me to report during the week for 3 days and then anchor the weekend news. That was a big deal for a young journalist just out of college. I took the job and we set a date to start.

There was a lot of talking with family and my wife about this major change, but I packed up my car, hooked on the U-Haul trailer, and my wife and I set out for Las Vegas. I didn't know if my marriage would work out, but I knew I had to try. I knew leaving the job in Green Bay might be putting my career in jeopardy, but saving my marriage seemed more important at the time. We all make decisions, and sometimes it's our heart talking and sometimes it's our head that is in charge.

The trip was long and hard. We went through Denver and up through the Rockies pulling a heavy trailer containing everything we owned. At every stop, she would call her boyfriend back in Green Bay. There was nothing I could do about it, but I kept pressing on believing that once we reached Las Vegas, everything would be fine. What was I thinking!

Las Vegas emerged from the desert in front of us as we crossed another mountain, and we followed the lines on the highway onto the Strip. I found a motel we could live in for a week or two until we could put some money down on an apartment, and I got ready to head to work at my new station. The newsroom was older and less organized than the one in Green Bay, and the people were not as friendly. I was welcomed by the news director (I can't recall his name) and he showed me around.

Then, he handed me a film camera, the ones that shot silent film, and told me he had a couple of assignments for me to handle. The man behind the assignment desk showed me where the keys were kept for the news cars parked out back. He said, "Take unit 7," and I grabbed the keys. I opened the door and the heat hit me. I was carrying a bag with the camera and extra film and a folder with notes on two meetings they wanted me to cover. I did my job that day. I got lost several times and I had a sinking feeling in my stomach that I had made a big mistake.

When I returned to the station, I reported to the news director, and I asked him about the anchoring duties that went along with my job descriptions. He said, "Oh, about that. We need to put that on hold for now. You just stick to reporting and I can't pay you the extra either for the anchoring." I was shocked. Remember this was at a time in the profession when we didn't sign contracts, so I didn't have a leg to stand on. I had driven thousands of miles, my loaded U-Haul trailer was still parked out behind the station, I had just put down a $500 deposit on a cheap apartment, my wife was still calling her boyfriend in Wisconsin, and my career was slowly falling apart.

The next morning, I reported for work and was again given a few assignments and a camera and the keys to unit 7, a 1977 beige AMC Gremlin. I headed off to do my job. As I parked the car in the lot next to an office building just off the Strip, I looked in the rear-view mirror and saw my face. I could not get out of the car. I realized I had made a colossal personal and professional mistake and if I didn't fix it, I would regret it forever.

Suddenly I didn't care about my marriage. I didn't care that I had made a commitment to the new station in Las Vegas. I knew I had to go back to Green Bay, get my old good job back, and reclaim my career and my dignity. It all happened while sitting in the ugliest car ever made, that beige Gremlin. I drove back to the station, walked in, and called my previous boss in Green Bay. He had been surprised that I had left and was happy to welcome me back. He said, "Ross, you can have your old job back if you are here in two weeks." I quit in Las Vegas that day. We hooked up the unpacked trailer, filled the gas tank, and headed east. We knew the route. I was going home.

I will never forget the major decision I made sitting in the front seat of that Gremlin. My first marriage didn't last, but my career did. When you find yourself in a Gremlin, tough decisions come much easier.

P.S.: I tell this story not to embarrass anyone. These kinds of personal stories help define us professionally. It helped me grow up and see the world differently and made me a better journalist.

New Year's Eve Las Vegas Strip with Cathy Ray

With Barbara Walters and Cathy Ray on the set of The View in Las Vegas

A BURNING CROSS AND A PARTY OF HATE

"The opposite of love is not hate, it's indifference. Fear is the only true enemy, born of ignorance and the parent of anger and hate."

—Louis C. K.

Fire changes things. It makes food better. It makes dark nights brighter and warmer. It also destroys and frightens. That is what this story is about, the night I was an uninvited guest at a Ku Klux Klan cross-lighting.

In the Los Angeles suburb of Lakeview Terrace, there isn't much excitement. It's a neighborhood of blue-collar values, soccer games for the kids after school, and usually quiet evenings. It was December 3, 1983, and I was working for KCBS-TV and had run into a story that was both dangerous and exciting.

I had been approached by a man named Peter Lake. Peter was a freelance journalist with a taste for danger. His previous claim to fame was locking himself in a cage underwater to videotape a killer shark. This next assignment would be more dangerous for him and for us.

Peter had infiltrated a national group of white supremacists. The Aryan Nation group was headquartered in Hayden Lake, Idaho, but its tentacles stretched nationwide. It was affiliated with the local Ku

Klux Klan chapters, including the one in southern California headed by Grand Dragon Tom Metzker. Peter had become the group's videographer and had convinced the members he could be trusted. He was our person "on the inside" while we worked to expose the tactics of this hate group from the outside looking in.

I have already written about my face-to-face encounter with Pastor Richard Butler, the head of the Aryan Nation group. He was competing with leaders of the Klan, the Aryan Brotherhood, and other smaller hate groups for members and money and attention. But, on one evening in Lakeview Terrace, they all came together to make a statement about their power to terrify.

Peter Lake sent word to me that they would all meet in the backyard of a supporter and light three crosses on fire. Cross-lightings have been used for decades to frighten Blacks in the south. The crosses would be lit in the front yard of a Black family or the supporter of that family. It was meant as a warning. This ceremony in Los Angeles was meant to send a message too, Lake told us. He said they wanted Blacks, Jews, and Asians in the area to know they were not welcome.

The crosses were scheduled to be doused with gasoline and lit just after sundown. I left the station in Hollywood with photojournalist Eliot Fons. We had worked together many times before, but we didn't know what to expect tonight. Lake told us that we would have to park several streets away and make our way to the hillside backyard by climbing up a steep slope in the back of the property. If we were seen, the ceremony organizers would be angry and he would not be able to protect us. He warned us to be careful.

Eliot and I made it to the property line as the sun was starting to set. We could see several men getting ready to pull ropes and lift the three big wooden crosses into holes dug in the ground. We hid in some thick bushes, trying to remain quiet. We saw them douse the sheet-wrapped hay bundles with gasoline and tie them to the crosses. We also saw our "insider", Peter Lake, videotaping it all up close. If they only knew.

We stayed hidden in the bushes, just 20 yards from the crosses. When it got dark, the men began coming out of the house and heading to the ceremony location. Some were dressed in leather jackets or T-shirts. We could see their faces. Others were covered head-to-toe with traditional Klan robes and masks. They gathered in a circle around the crosses. I heard the voice of Pastor Butler welcome everyone and thank them for the show of support. It was hard to hear everything from our spot in the bushes, but every few seconds there was cheering and applause. Then several men set the crosses on fire. We could feel the heat. The cheering got louder and louder.

We didn't dare even breathe. Some of the men were assigned as security and they had spread out along the property line. They had rifles and sidearms. One of them was standing about 15 feet in front of us with his back turned. Eliot had propped his camera next to a log and pointed it at the ceremony. Any movement by us might tip them off.

Then, suddenly, some of the men started running. There were shouts of "Police, run for it!" It seems the Los Angeles Police Department had been tipped off about the cross-lighting ceremony, too. Officers were crashing the party and making arrests. We didn't hesitate. Eliot grabbed his camera, and I had the microphone, and we jumped out the bushes and began videotaping the chaos and arrests. We had our LAPD press passes around our necks and we managed to stay out of the way for a minute or two, but then we were both grabbed from behind and handcuffed. I tried to plead with the officer and show him my pass, but he didn't have time to negotiate. He pushed me toward another officer who led Eliot and me to a row of squad cars on the street in front of the house. A sergeant finally came over and we were able to reason with him. He checked our press passes and ordered the handcuffs to be removed. Then he asked, "What the hell were you guys doing here and how did you know about it?"

I said, "Same way you did, Sergeant; someone tipped us off."

He took my business card and warned me that the department might want to see our videotape. I warned him back that it would take a subpoena. He was not happy.

Peter Lake was arrested that night, but the video he shot, and the video Eliot got hiding in the bushes, helped us show the real story of hate that night in southern California. That was just one of a series of stories we did about the Aryan Nation group and the Klan. Peter stayed in the group for another several months, reporting back to us daily and sharing videos.

I had always read about the life of Blacks in the South. To me it was a story in a history book. I had never experienced it but now I had, albeit in a different way. Now I can appreciate the fear felt by those who are the targets of these hate groups. I will never forget the heat on my face as those crosses burned.

A HORRIBLE HALLOWEEN

"The pain of grief is, perhaps, the price we pay for love."

—*Colin Murray Parkes*

When I bought my radio stations in Elizabethtown, Kentucky, I inherited a wonderful group of people who were dedicated to making it a success. We quickly became a family because we were collectively fighting for our survival. Everyone was involved; even family members sacrificed time on the weekends to attend live remote broadcasts or community festivals.

WRZI STAR 101.5 was a new radio station, and its ratings were non-existent. So, our sales team was always struggling to make a sale and my wife Linda was always struggling to make payroll. One of my jobs was to make the 45-minute drive to Louisville to meet with the regional advertising agencies to beg them to buy radio commercials from us. We had nothing more to offer than my smile and my enthusiasm.

On October 31, 1996, I loaded up my pamphlets and rate sheets and headed north.

Back at the station, Program Director Chris Landon was just finishing his morning shift on the air. Without Chris nothing would happen at STAR 101.5. He was the soul of the station. He planned the music every day and programmed the new computer that played music and commercials when we didn't have a live DJ. It was Chris's job to interpret the daily logs and make sure the advertisers got what they paid for. Chris sometimes did his job so quietly, we didn't even know he was at work. On the air, he was upbeat and funny and so professional. Off the air he was quiet and meek and willing to do whatever we needed to make the station a success. His wife and young son were always there, too. They would help us clean and just add life to our little operation. He ate his lunch in our lunchroom and usually headed home about two in the afternoon. On this Halloween, he also had his hard-earned paycheck.

I had a good meeting with Sheehy and Associates, one of the big agencies that represented Kroger grocery stores, and I was hoping a "buy" from them in November might help our bottom line. I was just getting in the car when my cell phone rang. It was the main switchboard at the station and I knew my stepdaughter, Amber, was on duty that day. I answered, "Hi, Girlie," all upbeat and excited, but I could tell right away from the sound of Amber's voice something was wrong.

"Are you on your way back?" she said.

"Yeah," I replied, "just got in the car. What's wrong?"

She told me that Chris Landon had been in a car accident and that our newsman, Ron Boone, was on the way to check it out to see how bad it was. He had heard it on the police scanner in the newsroom. My heart sunk.

"How bad is it?" I asked, knowing that she would not really know yet.

Amber said, "Ron left in tears; he said it didn't sound good."

I took a deep breath and told Amber to call me if she knew anything more. I hit the road heading south and I was very worried.

About halfway to Elizabethtown, my cell phone rang again. It was Amber calling, and when I answered, she was crying.

"Amber!" I insisted. "Please just tell me, what happened?"

I will never forget her exact words; she said, "Say a prayer, Papa; we lost Chris. He's gone."

It was about 4 pm when I pulled off the freeway and headed right for the emergency room at Hardin Memorial Hospital. That's where the ambulance took Chris after they cut him from his 1984 Impala. The impact had pushed the steering column back into his chest. According to the police, Chris was just driving south, heading out of town, when a woman in a white pickup pulled out of a bank parking lot. Instead of pulling into her lane heading north she crossed the centerline, hitting Chris head-on without warning. He had no time to react. He never regained consciousness. They found his paycheck on the front seat, along with a bag of candy for the kids he and his family expected at their door that Halloween evening.

When I walked into the emergency room, our entire staff was there. Ron Boone, who went to the scene, our sales team, Amber, my wife Linda. They were there, but there was nothing anyone could do. Chris was gone. The hospital chaplain led me into the room where Chris's wife Luann and their son Josh were sitting. They were in shock. They were alone. We were the only family they had in Elizabethtown.

I sat down next to Luann and grabbed her hand. Her eyes rose to mine. She said, "Ross, my beautiful man is gone. Why, Ross, why?" I just squeezed her hand and put my arm around her. I told her we were here for her and that no one would ever understand, but that she wouldn't be alone. I sat with her for about a half hour. She would cry and then stop. Their son, Josh, asked me if I knew what happened. I told him no, but I would find out and tell him everything he wanted to know. I also reminded him he was now the man of the family and he needed to be strong. This was going to be so hard for them.

I think it was nearly 8 o'clock that night before we left the hospital. Luann and Josh were staying with friends. The rest of the staff had gone home. I had to get up very early in the morning because I was the only one available to take Chris's place the next morning. *The Chris Landon Wake Up Show* would go on, but this time without Chris. I didn't know what I was going to do, but I knew I would figure it out and somehow Chris would help me.

I hardly slept. The alarm rang at 5 am and I just pulled on some jeans and headed for the station. It all felt so strange and sad and eerie. The Halloween decorations on the front steps had been partially ripped by the dew and the winds overnight. I turned on the lights, made some bad coffee, and got ready to spend the next three hours trying to be upbeat and give our listeners what Chris would have done had that woman not decided to take the wrong medication and pass out behind the wheel of her truck while she pulled out of the bank parking lot. She didn't know what happened either, but she survived the crash.

I knew I had to say something at six that morning when I cracked the microphone and started the show. I spent about a minute telling the listeners about the accident and about our loss of Chris Landon. I dedicated the show to him. He had a relationship with the people who tuned in every morning. I wanted them to know that we understood they were hurting too.

Before I went on the air, I really didn't have time to check what music Chris had loaded into the computer for the morning show. He had meticulously added the new playlist the day before, just before leaving. It was the last thing he had done for WRZI STAR 101.5.

I finished my explanation of what happened and how we had lost Chris. There was a big lump in my throat as I said, "Now let's get to some music." When I pressed the button, I glanced over at the computer screen. The music began and I could not believe my eyes or my ears. Coming out of the big speakers in the studio that Chris had called home was the song he had selected as his first one of the morning show. It was the one he would have played if he had not been killed just hours before. Now, every time I hear it, I think of Chris. The song that brought tears to my eyes again was Billy Joel's "Only the Good Die Young". Somehow, Chris knew it would be a horrible Halloween.

AN EXPLOSION OF EMOTION

"Violence is the last refuge of the incompetent."

—Isaasc Asimov

There is no mistaking the sound of an explosion. I was sitting at my kitchen table in my west side Indianapolis apartment, and the window was open because it was a hot, muggy September evening. It was quiet in the room. I was writing checks and paying bills after a day of work at WTHR. I was a reporter working for Channel 13, and the big story that fall of 1978 was a series of mysterious explosions in trash bins in the town of Speedway, home of the Indianapolis Motor Speedway. So far, no one had been injured, but people were scared. They didn't know who was doing it and why.

I could barely hear the traffic on the freeway about two blocks from my apartment and, occasionally, I could make out a dog barking somewhere. Then, there was a muffled boom. I didn't just hear it, I felt it in the pit of my stomach. It was not a loud boom, but I sat up straight in my dining room chair and froze. It was an explosion, and I knew, instinctively, that it was another one of the mysterious bombings.

I called the WTHR assignment desk. The night editor had not heard any radio calls, but he promised to check on it. For a moment, I felt the fear we had been talking about daily on our newscasts. It was an uneasy feeling of being unsafe. Then, my home phone rang again. When I answered, the assignment editor had a different tone. He said, "It was an explosion, and this time there are injuries. I need you to go. It's near your apartment. The police are staging at Speedway High School." I hung up and ran to get dressed.

I was on the scene in about 15 minutes, and it was chaos. Our photographer had not yet arrived, so I parked my car just outside the yellow police tape and headed for a group of people in the parking lot of the high school. Many were crying. They told me a man had picked up a duffle bag left next to his car, and it exploded. He was hurt badly and so was his wife. The freshman football game was over, and the parking lot was full of people.

The police were not saying if this "bomb" was connected to the other explosions that had everyone afraid, but there was no doubt what people at the school were thinking. They told me they were terrified. They said they were afraid to let their children play outside. It was terrorism, and no one knew why it was happening.

Carl Delong had his right leg blown off by the blast. He had survived Vietnam, only to face violence just blocks from his own home. The Speedway High School bomb was the last one of the series, but at the time, the people of Speedway didn't know that. They lived in fear for weeks, wondering when or if another one would explode somewhere.

The rest of this story is a complicated one involving a young man from Indianapolis who was found guilty of setting these explosions as a diversion. Police were closing in on his marijuana smuggling operation, and he had planted the bombs to try to distract them. Brett Kimberlin was eventually caught, tried, and sentenced to prison. I stayed on the story, even traveling to west Texas to see the makeshift airstrip he used to land planes filled with illegal marijuana. He is now free again after serving his sentence in a federal prison.

It was my first taste of what we now call "domestic terrorism". I heard the bomb go off that quiet September evening and then I felt the fear of people in Speedway, Indiana, wondering if their world would ever be safe again. I wondered, too.

BISCUITS AND GRAVY

"To me, food is as much about the moment, the occasion, the location and the company as it is about the taste."

—Heston Blumenthal

Sometimes it's not the story that you remember, it's the food.

In the late 1970s, I was a young reporter working for WTHR-TV in Indianapolis. It was December of 1977, and the coal miners' union decided to go on strike. Southern Indiana is full of coal mines and miners, so this became a major local story.

We left the station very early one very cold morning, heading for the union coal mine. It was dark when we left and all we had was coffee to keep us awake and warm. WTHR photojournalist Pat Thatcher was a veteran, and I was glad to have him manning the CP-16 film camera. We knew the miners could be a difficult bunch, especially when they were on strike.

Many didn't see the media as their friend. Many were just tough, hardworking coal miners who didn't like outsiders from Indianapolis invading their rural neighborhoods.

We made great time and arrived near the mine entrance about an hour before the first scheduled shift change. That is when the first picket lines were supposed to appear and when we could get our first reactions. Pat and I were sitting in the news car with the engine running and the heater blowing full blast. It was below freezing. He turned to me and said, "I'm hungry. Let's get something to eat." He put the car in gear and headed back toward the main road. He said, "I am dying for some hot biscuits and gravy!"

I had no idea what he was talking about. I had never heard of biscuits and gravy! I said, "What the hell is that?"

Pat looked at me like I was crazy. "You have never had biscuits and gravy?"

"Nope," I said. "Don't know what they are, but I am willing to try anything."

Growing up in Wisconsin, we had cheese curds and beer for breakfast sometimes, but never biscuits and gravy. It's traditionally a southern dish, and this was my first time living outside of Wisconsin, so I was learning all kinds of new things. We pulled into the snow-covered parking lot of the restaurant and, with a sly smile, Pat said, "Wait here, I will get you some biscuits and gravy."

This coal miners' strike was a big deal. It was not just Indiana miners. This was what they called a "wildcat" strike of miners in several midwestern states. It was clear the union leadership had little control over the men, and that made it dangerous. This was "life and death" for the workers, and no one knew how far they would go to make their point.

I saw Pat push the door open and walk toward the car. He was carrying a brown paper bag, like the kind we used to get at the grocery store. He jumped in and put the bag between us.

"Let's get back to the mine road," he said. "Then we will dig in."

The car filled with the smell of sausage. That's what it smelled like to me. During the short ride back to the mine, Pat was amazed again that I had never tasted biscuits and gravy. He said it was a staple in his home when he was growing up, and it reminded him of his family.

We stopped at the mine entrance. No one was there yet. Pat opened the paper bag and handed me a plastic fork and a Styrofoam food container. It was hot on the bottom, but it felt good in the cold. I opened the lid and, for the first time, saw biscuits and gravy. It was gray.

OH! It smelled great, but it was just a pile of gray slop. Pat said, "Dig in," and I did. Cautiously at first, but after the first couple of bites I was hooked. It was delicious! A young man from Wisconsin who moved to Indiana was now becoming more of a southern food lover.

We finished our breakfast just as the cars of the striking miners began to arrive. We put on our caps and gloves and got our gear from the truck and began working. Our stomachs were full.

The strike was very violent. It lasted over 3 months. During another one of our trips to cover the strike action, the tires on our news vehicle were slashed in a union headquarters parking lot. The miners were feeling the pressure and didn't want the media to see it. The strike lasted more than a year. It was a good story, but mostly, that day, it was a good breakfast. It's one I will never forget. Food always sticks with you.

DON'T CONFUSE ME WITH THE FACTS

"The ability to simplify means to eliminate the unnecessary so that the necessary may speak."

—*Hans Hofmann*

Bill Dean was a character and he told me something one day in the newsroom that I will never forget.

Bill was my news director in the late 1970s at WTHR in Indianapolis. He was a veteran who began his career working with Al Primo and the original Eyewitness News in Philadelphia. Bill was eccentric. He scoured the newspapers for stories and ads for vodka on sale. He drove a Boss 302 Mustang and kept the keys in his pocket. In fact, it was the sound of those keys jingling that always told us Bill was nearby. His nervous energy was transferred to the hand in his pocket where he shook those keys constantly. Bill Dean was a gem, and he would have done anything for us.

The newsroom was filled with reporters, some veterans, but most of us were young. This was my second job out of college, and I was honored to work in the 24th TV market in the nation. I had to work hard every day just to keep up with the others who had years of experience. Bill was always there to help me.

It was late afternoon on a Thursday, and I was at my desk in the open newsroom. We still used typewriters to compose our scripts and I was struggling to meet my deadline. I don't remember the specific story, but it was complicated, and my notebook was filled with names and numbers. I had to somehow distill it all into a TV news story in the next 90 minutes. I was panicking.

The newsroom was frenetic. Reporters, producers, photographers, and the support team were racing to get the news on the air. I was the only one, it seemed, who was sitting still and staring at my notebook. I was frozen, my fingers were on the typewriter keys, but they were not moving.

Then I heard his voice. Bill Dean had come out of his office and was standing near the newsroom door behind me. He yelled, "Becker! Are you gonna make the show?" *That's all I need!* I thought. *Now I have the boss pressuring me, too.*

I yelled back, "I hope so. It's a complicated story."

Then Bill spoke the words I would never forget, and that I share with young reporters. He said, "Becker, don't confuse me with the facts; just tell me a story!" He turned and walked away.

I took a deep breath and thought about what he had just yelled across the newsroom. "Just tell me a story." OK, I can do that, and I began writing. As I did, the words just flowed, and I began weaving in the information and facts I had spent the day gathering. It was a story, not a report. It had people in it and a plot. Bill had freed up my mind to get past the facts and create something that would help viewers understand the issue.

I now consider them magic words of advice. They worked for me that day in the WTHR newsroom, they work for me today and I have had some of my colleagues with whom I have shared this story say those words of wisdom work for them too when they got stuck. "Don't confuse me with the facts; just tell me a story!" is a quote that inspired me to call myself a storyteller.

The facts are crucial to every story. We must get them right and they must be put in context. But it is also our job to weave them into the story that viewers and readers can understand and appreciate. That is what Bill Dean taught me with his words yelled across the newsroom. Sometimes yelling does get your attention.

FLYING BLIND

"Life is either a daring adventure or nothing at all."

—*Helen Keller*

Sometimes it is better not to know the risks before you dive into an assignment.

In 1976, I was working as a reporter for WFRV-TV in Green Bay. It was summertime, and that means fire season in the millions of acres of forest in the viewing area. A fire broke out in the upper peninsula of Michigan, and I was sent to cover it. I got there ok. I got the story, but I nearly didn't make it home.

We usually worked in teams at WFRV. The photographer would handle the film gear, camera, and lights. I would do the reporting, but this time I was a "one-man band". The assignment desk arranged for me to fly in a chartered small plane that would land at a small airport near the fire, and then I would rent a car and get the story. It was going to be my first time in a small prop-driven airplane, and I was excited.

The flight to the story was exciting and smooth. We landed at the small airport, and I even shot film of the giant smoke plume from the fire as we were turning to aim for the runway. I only had a few hours on the ground to get the story, and when I returned to the airport, the pilot was waiting. He was a young man about my age, early twenties with a "flat top" haircut. He was quiet and deeply focused on his job. He checked out the plane and went through the safety procedures with me. I was in a hurry, of course. I had a deadline. It did not seem to matter to this young man. He asked me to sit in the front seat with him instead of in the back. He was all business.

As we took off, it was sunny and clear, but he told me over the headsets that we might run into some weather as we get closer to Green Bay. It was about a 2-hour flight, so I settled in and began writing and organizing my story about the fire. My mind was racing. We had to "soup" the film (develop it using a machine), and then I would edit it using a film viewer and glue. We had to make two reels, one for the video and one for the sound. They would roll at the same time on two different projectors and the director would switch between them to make the story look complete on-the-air. That is why we still call it an "A-roll" and a "B-roll".

About an hour into the flight, the pilot said, "Ross, would you help me with something as we prepare to land?" I said, of course. He wanted me to take out my notebook and listen carefully to what the air traffic controllers were saying to him. He said, "Write it all down; it's critical." Outside the window of the tiny 4-seater airplane, it was milky white. The clouds had enveloped the plane, and it was beginning to rain on the windshield.

I looked over at the young pilot and his eyes were as big as poker chips. He was focusing on the dashboard and glancing out the front window even though there was nothing to see. He was flying using instruments only. Pilots are trained to do that, and I hoped he was good at it.

Each plane has an ID number. The one I was in had N2287B. I had headphones on with a built-in microphone and I was listening for that number. It was my cue to write down the info and make sure we didn't miss anything. That air traffic controller was our eyes, since we could not see anything inside the plane. "Cessna Nancy 2287 Baker, turn right fifteen degrees and maintain heading" crackled in my ears. I pressed the microphone button and asked the pilot if he got it. He said yes. I glanced at him, and he was sweating. He never looked back at me.

"Nancy 2287 Baker, you are three miles from the runway; begin your descent." The pilot reached over to the throttle levers and began to slow the plane down. He pointed the nose down and I could feel myself slide forward slightly in the seat. We could see nothing out the windshield. It was white. It was an eerie feeling.

Then the radio crackled again and this time the tone in the voice was urgent. "Cessna N2287B, what is your altitude?" The pilot answered immediately. The air traffic controller came right back and this time I could tell he was flustered. "Make an immediate right turn and drop to seven thousand feet."

The pilot shouted to me over the intercom, "Did he say seven thousand feet?"

I said yes, and the pilot yanked the yoke to the right and pulled back on the throttle lever. We turned and headed down, quickly.

Now I was sweating, too. It was frightening. The tone of the air traffic controller's voice was what scared me the most. We were clearly in danger, but we couldn't see anything. The controller came back on the radio using our call sign and said, "You are on the same path as a jetliner coming into the airport and I need you to keep dropping quickly or you will collide." *What?!* I heard it! I looked out the windshield and all I saw was fog and rain. I looked at the pilot and he was pale. We both sat there waiting to be obliterated by a jetliner heading to the same place we were headed.

It seemed like an hour, but it was only 4 minutes later that we broke through the clouds and fog and saw the end of the runway at Austin Straubel Field in Green Bay. The pilot aimed for the runway. We touched down and began rolling toward the hangar. I was exhausted and relieved. I asked the young pilot, "Were you scared?" He looked at me and just shook his head.

Then he said something I will never forget: "I trained to fly by instrument, but until today I had never done it for real. That was my first time!"

It was my maiden voyage in a small plane and, now I found out it was the first time my pilot had ever flown by instrument. That is why he asked me to help him. I am glad I didn't know that while we were still in the air.

When we pulled up to the hangar, I said thank you. We both looked at each other and started laughing. It was nervous laughter. We were glad to be on the ground.

In the few days after my crazy flight, I thought about the times in my career when I was faced with a challenge I had never faced before, and I remembered the young pilot. He didn't fail either. He did it and I was along for the ride.

FROZEN BY FIRE

"Never regret. If it's good, it's wonderful. If it's bad, it's experience."

—*Jean Plaidy*

O nce you see something horrible, you can never erase it from your memory.

In 1984, I worked for KCBS in Los Angeles and didn't know that the images and stories of what happened in Mexico that November Monday morning would stay with me forever. When I got to the newsroom, I was immediately told to get ready to fly to Mexico City. A huge liquified petroleum gas facility near Mexico City had exploded and the fireball created burned through a nearby slum neighborhood. It was horrible. The death toll was rising by the hour.

When we landed, we discovered it would be a 45-minute drive to the disaster zone. The boys selling newspapers on the curb along the way were yelling the headline, just two words: "Fuego Mortal", or "Deadly Fire". Forty thousand people lived in the town of San Juan Ixhuatepec, a poor suburb of Mexico City, and home to the largest liquified petroleum gas plant in the country. Most of the men living in town were either farmers or they worked at the gas plant. As we got closer, we were forced to stop and walk. The roads were jammed with people. Some were walking out of the area with shocked and stunned looks on their faces. Some carried knapsacks or blankets tied at the top. Others were walking with us, heading into the fire zone. They were scared. They needed to find their loved ones.

We came at the top of a hill and saw the valley below. There was no color. Gray smoke was billowing from the fires still burning at the plant in the distance. The neighborhood next to it was gone, except for the walls of charred homes. These were not big houses; they were adobe shacks with wooden doors and plywood roofs. Police were trying to keep people away, but it was no use. It was impossible to secure the huge area, and local officials told us they didn't know how they were going to get to and identify the dead. This was a huge crime scene, but we were waved on in and that is when the story changed. We didn't come to the story; it came to us in a very dramatic way.

We started walking down one of the burned-out streets. Everything was touched by the flash fire. The trees were black and bare. The cars were gray and gutted. Even the seats were gone. Just charred metal springs remained. We walked up to a man sitting on the curb in front of one of the houses. We asked him in Spanish, "Is this your house?" He said no, it was his brother's house.

"Where is he?" I asked. He said he was inside and gestured for me to walk in the front door. There was no door. It had been burned from the hinges. The man followed behind me and my photographer led the way. As we approached the end of the hallway entrance, the photographer stopped and turned to the room on the right. I slipped behind him and saw a family frozen by fire. The sofa was just a metal frame and on it were three bodies. They were black, charred remains of three humans caught in the conflagration. They had no time to move. The fire came like a flash flood.

I just stood there, not believing my eyes. I turned to the man who we met outside, and he nodded and said in Spanish, "That's my brother and his family. They had nowhere to run."

Back outside again, we kept walking and found children looking for their missing parents. We found women sifting through the black, dust looking for mementos. In virtually every house or backyard we saw bodies. They were burned beyond recognition. It was even hard to tell if they were men or women. We could tell the children only because they were smaller.

The real story I want to share is what I saw in the eyes of those we met wandering the streets here. They were emotionally stunned, just like we were. They were seeing death everywhere and becoming immune to it.

There is no accurate count of how many died in this industrial accident. The initial number was 248 people killed. However, we went back to the neighborhood several years later to investigate reports that the government buried more than 1,000 victims in a hillside nearby. The houses were being rebuilt. The people were moving back in and, surprisingly, the huge liquid petroleum plant was still there, back in operation right next door.

But the images from that day were frozen in my mind. Frozen by fire.

VIEW OF BURNED-OUT NEIGHBORHOOD NEXT TO MEXICAN GAS PLANT

JESUS OR SUPERMAN?

"It's great to be great, but it's greater to be human."

—*Will Rogers*

If you want humanity, ask a human question. I learned that lesson in a very embarrassing moment in 1985 while working as a reporter for KCBS in Los Angeles.

It was midday on a Thursday and the Catholic Diocese of Los Angeles issued a press release. A new archbishop had been named and it was a big deal. A bishop from Stockton was going to be the new leader of the church in southern California.

The assignment desk called me and ordered me back to the station to prepare for a flight to Stockton to interview Bishop Roger Mahony. He was born in Hollywood and grew up in the San Fernando Valley and would now face the biggest challenge of his life.

Photojournalist Larry Greene and I headed to the airport, landing two hours later in Fresno. We rented a car and headed for the bishop's office. He greeted us with a big smile. He was one of those people who made you feel instantly comfortable, yet he was all business, and he seemed a bit overwhelmed by the media attention.

I had prepared the best I could with the limited time I had. We had a great research department at KBCS headed by Lorraine Hillman. She prepared a file of background information about Mahony and his roots in the Los Angeles area. I also read about the controversies facing the church and how they might affect local Catholics. I was ready when we hit the ground in Fresno.

Larry set up the lights and camera in Mahony's small office while he was out of the room. When he walked in and sat down, the lights came on and the camera rolled. We talked about his background and how he would make the changes some say were necessary in the Los Angeles diocese. We talked about women in the priesthood and immigration. He had just learned of his new job hours earlier and he told me he was just getting his head around his new assignment. He was nice and direct, but there was something missing in the interview. Yet, after about 15 minutes of questioning, I said, "Thank you, Bishop Mahony," and turned to Larry to ask him to turn off the camera.

Larry said, "No, not yet." He had one more question. I was shocked! Larry had a great sense of humor and was always pulling practical jokes and I feared this was another one in front of the new archbishop. Larry said, "Bishop Mahony, if Jesus and Superman were in a fight, who would win?"

It was classic Larry, and I was mortified. But it turned out to be a brilliant question. For the first time in the interview Mahony's face lit up. With a huge smile he said, "Well, I never really thought about it, but I would have to say Jesus, because that's my job." His smile was as genuine as his answer. We laughed together. It showed him as a real person and not just a religious leader in a black robe.

Larry accomplished what I could not accomplish with my prepared questions. He exposed the humanity in a man who was trained to be restrained and professional. Larry asked a human question, and he exposed the real person. If you want humanity, ask a human question. That is what I learned that day.

Archbishop Mahony led the church in L.A. for more than two decades. Every time I saw him, I remembered Larry's question and Mahony's answer. It reminded me to break the barrier of what is expected and ask the unexpected.

PHOTOJOURNALIST LARRY GREENE WITH HIS FRIEND

MY FRIEND, THE MURDERER

"Growing apart doesn't change the fact that for a long time we grew side by side; our roots will always be tangled."

—*Ally Condie*

In January of 1975, a beautiful young woman was murdered. She was home in the Green Bay, Wisconsin, area for the holidays and was at a New Year's Eve party. She made the wrong choice that night, but it should not have cost her her life. Her name was Susan Reignier. When I began researching for this story on social media, I was contacted by some of her family and friends. They wanted her to be remembered for her smile and her spirit. The man who killed her was *my* friend, and I ended up in the courtroom one day during his murder trial as a reporter.

His name was Dickey. That's what we called him in high school. His last name is not important to this story, and I don't want to give him the satisfaction of having his crime sensationalized in print. He was not the most popular kid in school, by far. In fact, he was a little quiet and maybe even shy. My best buddy, Joe, and I would sometimes drive by and pick up Dickey when we went out on a Saturday night. He was in our class, and he lived in our neighborhood. He was just like our other friends, or at least we thought so.

After we graduated Preble High School, I went off to college and lost touch with Dickey. Turns out that was a good thing. My first journalism job after college graduation was back in Green Bay. I got the chance to report for WFRV-TV in my hometown. It was May of 1975. One of the stories on our coverage list for the month of June was a murder trial. A woman's body was found in January on the ice of Ashwaubenon Creek. Police said the man arrested for her murder confessed but was pleading not guilty by reason of insanity or diminished capacity.

Another reporter was assigned to cover the trial, so I wasn't paying much attention to the details. It was my first job out of college, and I was focusing on the stories I had to tackle. However, one day the reporter assigned to the murder trial called in sick and I had to step in. When I saw the formal name of the man on trial, I wondered if it was the same guy I knew in high school. It was a common last name. It couldn't be. Could it?

When I arrived at the Brown County Courthouse that morning, I headed upstairs to the courtroom. There were a few people already there, but no defendant. I sat down with my notebook and waited. A few minutes later, the side door opened. Two deputies led him in. He was dressed in an orange jail jumpsuit. I was shocked. It was him. My high school friend Dickey was handcuffed and facing 25 years to life for murder. I was in the front row of the courtroom and Dickey did a double take. I was staring at him. Our eyes met. He shuffled over to the table and before sitting down he said, "Hi, Ross." That was it.

It was my first real court case as a reporter and my first taste of a murder trial (I would cover hundreds more). Dickey had picked up the girl, who was hitchhiking home from a New Year's Eve party and stabbed her. He dumped her body on the creek bed. I never found out the motive for this brutality.

I reported on what happened in court that day and the next day the other reporter was back on the case. I went on to something else, but I never forgot the look on Dickey's face when he saw me, or the feeling in my heart.

The guy we hung around with as high school students was sent away to prison. Do you really know the people who you call friends or acquaintances?

One of the people who posted a comment recently when I was working on researching this story said, "She (the victim) was my friend. I never use the word hate but I hate the boy who took her life!" We all do, even his friends who end up being reporters.

Author note: This story appeared first on my mentoring website TvNewsmentor.com.

https://tvnewsmentor.com/my-friend-the-murderer/

I used it as a teaching tool for young reporters who find themselves dealing with friends or family when reporting.

A RED, WHITE, AND BLUE DIAPER

"The only difference between genius and insanity is that genius has its limits."

—*Albert Einstein*

Larry Flynt is a character, a protestor, a pervert by his own admission, a drug addict, an instigator, a promoter, and a master manipulator. He is the founder of *Hustler* magazine, which, during the 1980s, the U.S. government called pornography. It started a war, and I got caught in it.

In 1983, Flynt obtained a grainy black-and-white videotape showing auto company owner John DeLorean looking at a briefcase full of cocaine in a hotel room near Los Angeles International Airport. It was an FBI sting operation. DeLorean could be heard saying, "It's good as gold." The agents claimed DeLorean took the bait and was ready to buy the $24 million worth of drugs and resell them to financially save his car empire. Flynt gave the videotape to KCBS-TV on a Sunday and it first aired on *60 Minutes*. Government prosecutors claimed making the tapes public jeopardized their case and the government demanded to know how this magazine publisher obtained this FBI-generated surveillance video. Flynt refused to tell them, claiming protection under the First Amendment. The battle was on and, as we all found out again, Flynt never played by the rules.

As a reporter for KCBS, I was assigned to cover the court battle. A federal courtroom is a sanctuary. The rules are strict. There are no cameras allowed inside, so we had our courtroom artist there for Flynt's hearing. He was charged with contempt of court for not revealing the source of the DeLorean video. He was ordered to show up and pay his daily fine, $10,000, or reveal his source.

We were all gathered inside the courtroom. The room was mostly filled with reporters. The federal prosecutor was sitting with his team at the table in front. The big double doors in the back of the room opened and we could hear his voice immediately. Flynt was already talking, taunting, laughing. His laugh sounded more like a cackle. Behind the two security guards leading him, we saw him sitting in his wheelchair (he needed the chair because of an injury suffered years earlier in an assassination attempt). He was wearing a bulletproof vest with a purple heart pinned to it, and instead of pants he was wearing a diaper constructed from the U.S. flag. He said, "If they are gonna shit on my rights, I am gonna help them shit on the flag." It was his protest, and it was a bold move even for him.

They rolled him up to the defense table where he met his lawyers. The attorneys were obviously caught off-guard by their client's antics, but Flynt would not be silenced. He growled that he should be protected by the First Amendment, and he said he was here to pay the fine for contempt. A man behind him had a white cloth bag. Flynt said it was full of money.

Federal Judge Robert Takasugi came into the courtroom as the bailiff shouted, "All, please rise." He asked Flynt to reveal the source. Flynt said he was the publisher of *Hustler* magazine and was a member of the press protected by the First Amendment. The judge imposed the fine and that's when Flynt asked his helper to open the white bag. Inside was cash. He said there was $10,000 in small bills. The judge was smiling. Flynt said he would continue to show up every day to pay the fine, and next time he would bring pennies.

Takasugi ordered Flynt, personally, to count the money for the court clerk, and that added to the bizarre court hearing. It took a long time, and during the counting Flynt kept talking and the judge kept asking for order in the court. There was Flynt, dressed in a red, white, and blue diaper, wearing a bulletproof vest and a borrowed Purple Heart, counting stacks of $1 bills. He brought eight thousand $1 bills and paid the rest in $5, $10, and $20 bills. When the hearing was over, we met him on the sidewalk outside. He was clearly loving the attention and the protest. He was putting on a show to make his point and it worked.

A few days later, the judge granted Flynt immunity from prosecution if he broke any law to get the videotapes. He was also ordered to testify before the grand jury hearing the DeLorean case. We never found out, for sure, who leaked the FBI video (he claimed it was someone nicknamed "the Samurai"). But Flynt was not immune from facing another charge. Within a few weeks, he was charged with another crime: desecration of the U.S. flag. You don't use one as a diaper in federal court without consequences.

It was clear this case, on both sides, was not about justice. It was about who would win the battle of publicity. It was an unfair fight. Flynt was a crazy master.

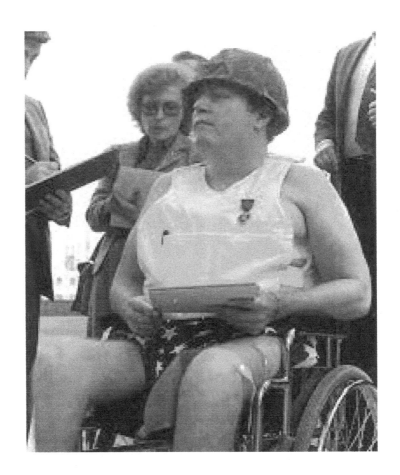

RIGHT PLACE, WRONG TIME

"Am I walking toward something I should be running away from?"

—*Shirley Jackson*

It's just not natural to hear gunshots inside a shopping mall. They echo, and so do the screams.

I had just finished my dinner salad in the newsroom at ABC4 in Salt Lake City. It was Valentine's Day 2007. I sat right in front of the assignment desk, and it was always noisy. The police radio scanners were turned up loud, and I tried to ignore them. Then, we heard it and could not mistake the urgency. The dispatcher was calm but forceful: "A man with a shotgun inside Trolley Square Mall, we have an active shooter, there are casualties."

I shot out of my desk chair and ran to the assignment desk counter. We were all stunned. Trolley Square was a high-end shopping mall on the north side of downtown Salt Lake City. We didn't wait for more info; I grabbed my bag and ran for the parking lot. The photographer met me there. We jumped in a van equipped with a microwave transmitter and headed for the mall. It was only a 5-minute drive.

During that drive I got more information. The shooter was pinned down inside by the police, and the desk had received a call from one of our reporters. She was inside shopping and was now trapped in a supply closet with other shoppers. She was on the phone and relaying what she heard through the door.

As we got close to the mall, the streets were jammed. There were cars filled with people trying to get away and there were police cruisers everywhere. Instead of waiting in the truck, I jumped out and told the photographer we would meet on the other side of the building. With my bag over my shoulder, I ran toward the east doors of the mall. There were police everywhere, some with their guns drawn, but they paid no attention to me. I ran right up to the mall door, grabbed the handle, and entered the food court area. I took two steps and froze. The gunshots echoed through the brick hallway leading up to the main floor. It was a pistol shot, then another. I ducked behind a planter near the door. We didn't have cellphones with video recorders, so I could not record anything, but I could listen. I heard yelling. I could not make out what was being said, but the tone was desperate.

Suddenly, one of the police officers ducking with me nearby decided I should not be there. He pointed and ordered me outside. I ran to the door and pushed it open. The cold air hit me. I stood there for a moment. I couldn't move. I ran around the outside of the building to the west parking lot, where all the TV station vehicles were parked. I put in my earpiece and called the station. I got a little more info from the assignment desk and found out that our reporter who was trapped inside was ok and heading for my location to do an interview. As always happens, the next few hours were a blur of live reports, phone calls, coaxing witnesses to talk, and answering questions from the anchors back at the station. I talked about my experience, but I still didn't have time to really process it. I had heard the two shots that killed the gunman. I had walked into the mall just moments before the police moved in on the man with the shotgun in the greeting card store. It was Valentine's Day, and the place was filled with people.

Five people were killed and four were wounded in the gunfire. Police never determined a motive. I will never forget the sounds. The gunshots and the yelling. I was in the right place at the wrong time. Every Valentine's Day, I think about those killed and wounded at that mall. They were trying to hide from the danger; I ran toward it.

WHO IS "ROSE BAKER"?

"For every good reason there is to lie, there is a better reason to tell the truth."

—*Bo Bennett*

"Rose Baker" is a made-up name. So is Ross Baker, Russ Becker, and three other names that look and sound a bit like Ross Becker. I used these made-up names in an investigative report for KCBS-TV in Los Angeles, and the story nearly got me charged with a federal crime.

I am still not sure I did the right thing, and when I was sitting in the office of the federal prosecutor with my lawyer (which the station didn't pay for), I was worried I had stepped over some legal or journalistic line. This decision still bothers me today. But I did expose a flaw in the election system in Los Angeles County.

It was the late 1980s, and election day was approaching. The ads on TV were really starting to get on everyone's nerves. I got a letter from a viewer claiming that people were planning to try to swing the election results by registering to vote multiple times. Since poll workers were not allowed to check official identification, the viewer claimed it was possible to trick them into allowing some people to vote more than once.

In the large countywide races, a few votes would not make a major difference, but in some of the smaller, local communities or school board races, several votes could sway an election. I wanted to find out if it was even possible for this multiple vote fraud to happen.

The L.A. County clerk insisted it was impossible. There are checks and balances, he told me in an interview. He refused to reveal those safeguards to protect the election counting process. I still wanted to test it.

I picked up six voter registration cards at the Hollywood post office and filled them out. Each name was a variation of my name. Not exact, but close. There was a reason for this. I put the addresses of colleagues at KCBS and asked them to give me any mail they received with the fake name attached. I got all six back with letters congratulating me on my voter registration and urging me to vote in the upcoming election. Each letter even had a voting location listed. The plan was, on election day, to go to each voting precinct with my registration card in hand and try to vote. My newsroom managers were on board.

The plan was elaborate. The desk would first send a photojournalist to a voting location, presumably to get a video of people voting for a general story. I would show up while the photographer was there, and they would record me checking in and going into a voting booth.

At stop number 1, I walked up to the woman at the check-in table and strongly announced, "Good morning, I am here to vote," and handed her my first card with the name "Rose Baker".

She looked at the card and then looked at me and said, "Rose?"

I smiled, then laughed and said, "No, it's Ross, but that happens all the time." She laughed too and checked the name "Rose Baker" on her master list and handed me a ballot. She said thanks for voting and pointed me to the voting booth.

Behind the curtain I didn't vote, but instead I wrote KCBS in big black letters on the punch card ballot. The plan was to make sure voter officials knew I didn't illegally vote or in any way affect the election outcome, but I wanted them to track the ballot with the fake name.

I left the voting booth, deposited my ballot in the official box, and left. I did the same thing five more times, and each time the voting monitors gave me a ballot, even though the name was wrong on the official list and allowed me to vote. We had video of it all. The story was coming together.

As the county-wide votes began coming in that night, I was on the air with the KCBS team reporting the outcome of our investigation. We confronted the Los Angeles County clerk about our investigation, and he located the KCBS-marked ballots in the official counting bins. He was furious. He believed what we did didn't prove anything! I believed we demonstrated how someone could vote more than once under the current system with no official identification needed. The story aired during our "live" election night coverage, and our station management loved it.

About a week later, the news director called me in and told me I had to meet with a federal prosecutor about my story. There was some concern that I had, intentionally, tried to defraud the election process with my scheme. The county clerk was so angry that I exposed the flaw, he demanded action.

My lawyer and I met with the prosecutor, who told me I had broken a federal law. I had lied on a federal election document and that, if convicted, I could be sent to federal prison. It was serious. I explained that I didn't actually vote and that, as a journalist, I was working to demonstrate the truth about the system. My lawyer asked me to leave the room. He wanted a private conversation with the prosecutor.

When I was asked back in, the prosecutor looked at me and said, "Don't do this again. Next time I won't be able to look the other way!"

I was off the hook.

On the way back to the station, my lawyer, George Bane, told me he reminded the prosecutor that a public trial would be covered by the station, and did they really want even more people to know that the voting system was flawed. He warned them of an even larger backlash and the feds backed down.

I still wonder if what I did was right. I know my intentions were pure, but I did break the law. But I am not losing any sleep over it. Anymore.

RUNNING TOWARD THE DANGER

"When the whole world is running towards a cliff, he who is running in the opposite direction appears to have lost his mind."

—C. S. Lewis

When you are covering a story, sometimes you don't think, you just react. Only when the crisis moment is over do you have time to reflect on what you did. I had one of those moments while covering the state funeral for President Ronald Reagan.

I was playing golf with a friend in San Diego when I got the phone call. Former President Ronald Reagan was dead. His age and his Alzheimer's disease finally took him. My news director at KTNV-TV in Las Vegas said, "Get home as soon as possible; we have you on a red-eye flight to Washington D.C." It would be the start of three long days of work that would be filled with emotion.

We were set up in our "live" reporting location on the National Mall looking east toward the U.S. Capitol building. We were joined by hundreds of other reporters and photographers from around the world. The former president's body would be brought to the Capitol and laid down in state while thousands filed past the casket. The Capitol police were already setting up the barriers that would form the lines into the building. It was a maze of metal fencing leading to the doors of the building.

It was hot and humid. Ninety degrees with 90 percent humidity and, occasionally, we would be drenched by a downpour. We were tired, too. Each day was filled with seemingly endless "live" reports in every newscast we had on the air. In between, we were interviewing people gathering to pay their respects to the former president.

On the second day, we had just finished a "live" report for our noon newscast in Las Vegas. It was already almost 4:30 in the afternoon on the east coast. Suddenly, there was a buzz in the crowd of reporters and photographers and everyone was looking toward the Capitol building.

People who had been in line to see the former president were running toward us. They were scared. Hundreds of them were coming at us. Some women were carrying their children. Fathers, too. I grabbed my briefcase and yelled to my photographer, "Let's go!" We took off up the hill toward the building, fighting the crowd like salmon swimming upstream. Something was happening, but we didn't know why everyone was so scared. I saw a Capitol security guard running toward me. I grabbed his arm and said, "What is going on?" He said they were evacuating the Capitol because an unidentified plane was in the area and it might be a terrorist attack.

He turned and ran away. I kept running toward the building. We got to the steps and froze. The police had taken the metal barriers used to marshal people and turned them into a blockade. I tried to call the station in Las Vegas, but our cell phones were dead. The authorities had turned off the cell towers in the area to try to stop the possible terrorists.

It was at that moment it occurred to me that while everyone else was running from danger, we were running toward it, along with scores of other reporters and photographers. We kept looking at the sky, wondering if a jetliner flown by terrorists was going to slam into the building, just like it had on 9/11. What the hell were we doing there? We would be killed! We never really thought about it until we were too close to do anything about it.

There were bells ringing and sirens screaming inside and outside the iconic building. There is a procedure for evacuating the Capitol, and it worked. In a matter of minutes, the place was empty, except for a few guards, the body of a former president, and about 50 reporters and photographers milling around on the steps outside. We just stood there looking at the sky, but nothing happened.

It was a false alarm. A small plane carrying Ernie Fletcher, then governor of Kentucky, who was arriving for the funeral, was preparing to land at nearby Reagan National Airport. The plane had been cleared to land but had radio problems that prevented communication with the air traffic controllers. Air Force fighter jets were dispatched to intercept the unidentified plane, and that's what triggered the chaos, the evacuation, and fear of a terrorist threat on Capitol Hill.

As we walked back to our "live" report location about two blocks away on the National Mall, everyone in our group was quiet. I was reflecting on what had just happened. What if this had not been a false alarm? I also found something out about myself and my colleagues. We didn't even flinch when the people came running toward us; we started running toward them and the story. The potential danger didn't cross our minds, until later. I was not alone. Reporters, photographers, producers, and those who call themselves members of the "media" are first responders, too.

The rest of the time in Washington D.C. was a blur of sweltering heat, patriotism, tears, and pageantry as the funeral for the former president unfolded. I remember standing on Constitution Avenue amid a crowd of people as the president's casket rolled by. At that moment, three fighter jets flew overhead as a tribute. I wondered if they were the same pilots who had responded to try to keep us all safe just 24 hours earlier.

SATANIC PANIC AND A MEXICAN STANDOFF

*"Now I know that anytime you see a 'no trespassing' sign, it means
you've got to go in and take a look."*

—*Kyung-Sook Shin*

Tecate, Mexico, is just across the border from California. It's
not a big place, but it's known for the brewery that produces
Tecate brand beer. We found out it's not a good place to challenge the
local police.

It was 1983 and I was working for KCBS-TV in Los Angeles,
and we were facing one of the biggest stories and biggest journalistic
challenges of our professional lives. It was the McMartin preschool
molestation case, and I was the lead reporter. The McMartin preschool
was in Manhattan Beach, California, which is a beach suburb of Los
Angeles. The district attorney had arrested and filed child molestation
charges against the school owner, her son, and several teachers. Parents
were accusing them of sexually abusing and conducting satanic rituals
on hundreds of children who were students there. The parents were
demanding action, but the defendants and others were claiming it was
all a mistake and the methods for questioning some of the children
were called into question.

The community was panicking. In the newsroom we would get anonymous tip calls daily leading us in a new direction to look for evidence. One call wanted us to look for secret tunnels under the school where they supposedly led children to another location to abuse them. Another caller would claim they knew a local politician was involved and working to protect the McMartins. Parents would call claiming their son or daughter just revealed new information proving the teachers were guilty. We had to try to follow up on all of it. There were a lot of dead ends, but bottom line, the McMartins and the teachers were facing serious charges, and that could not be ignored.

One of the anonymous calls that came in began a series of events that led me and a photojournalist to head south across the border into Mexico. The caller claimed he was a worker at a bus company and that the McMartin family rented school buses from the company. Sometimes, he said, it was once a week. He said, in the middle of a school day, some of the children at the McMartin preschool were loaded into the bus and driven to the small Mexican town of Tecate. There, he said, the driver would drop the children off at an abandoned orphanage just outside of town, and there, he said, Mexican men would pay to "have their way" with the children. It was a crazy allegation, but we were in the middle of a crazy story and all of it was hard to believe. The decision was made—we must go check this out.

Photojournalist Ramon Nunez and I left the next morning for Tecate. The plan was to cross the border, go directly to the abandoned orphanage, shoot some video, and then do what's called a "stand-up". A stand-up is that moment in a TV news story when the reporter appears holding a microphone and says a sentence or two or shows you something to help you understand the story.

We drove into town and went right past the Tecate brewery. It was a very hot day and we talked about getting a beer when we were done. The orphanage was off one of the main roads leading south out of town at the end of a long gravel driveway.

There was no one there. We got out and I began looking in the windows. There was some worn furniture and some papers strewn on the floor, but not much else. Ramon was recording video of the building and the grounds and of me looking inside. I tested the doors. They were locked and I was not going to break in. If buses were arriving here with children, there was no evidence of that.

Then I noticed a dust cloud coming toward us down the long entrance driveway. It was a Tecate city police car with two officers inside. They got out and walked over and asked us for our identification. They spoke Spanish; I could not, so Ramon help with the translations. We explained we were from CBS in Los Angeles and just wanted some video of the building and grounds for a story. One of them said, "I know why you are here, but we need you to leave now. This is private property, and you are trespassing." I gently argued with the officers for a few minutes, while Ramon finished shooting what he needed. Then we packed up and left to go back to town. The officers got to the main road and turned the other way.

We decided to grab some lunch and during our break I decided I wanted to do a "stand-up" to explain what the anonymous caller had told us about this abandoned orphanage. It would mean going back to the property we had already been warned to stay away from. We decided it was worth the risk because, we thought, the police wouldn't do anything anyway. It was just trespassing.

This time when we pulled into the long driveway we only went halfway to the building. We got out and Ramon set up the camera and I stood on the side of the driveway preparing to deliver my lines. Suddenly, the Tecate police car was coming back and this time it was speeding down the gravel road. The officer driving slid to a stop and jumped out with his hand on his weapon. He said, "This is no longer a warning. I told you this is trespassing and now you are coming with us!"

We were ordered to get in the news car and follow the officers to the Tecate police station. We parked right in front. It was a small, stucco building with two windows. One of the windows was open. I could see the curtains blowing in the breeze. The other window was glass, but it had bars on the outside. The front door had bars too. We were led inside, and I was put in the room with the bars on the window. There was no air-conditioning. It was sweltering hot. Since he spoke Spanish, Ramon said he was being taken into the back office to talk to the chief of police. They wanted to arrest us for trespassing, and he had to try to talk them out of it.

I sat there sweating for about an hour. Finally, the door opened, and Ramon was there by himself. He said, "Let's go, now!" and we both pushed the main door open and walked quickly to the CBS news car parked out front.

Just as Ramon was starting the engine, the chief came out and knocked on the car window. He said, "Dirigete a la frontera y sigue conduciendo y no regreses!"

Ramon put the car into gear, made a U-turn, and took off. I asked him what the chief said. Ramon said, "Head for the border and keep driving and don't come back!" Ok, we got the message.

The crazy story about the orphanage was just one of hundreds we checked out before during and even after the McMartin Preschool molestation trial. In early 1990, those charged were all found not guilty on most of the charges. The judge declared a mistrial on several others and dismissed one charge of conspiracy. The case had cost the county

$15 million. In the end, one of the parents who originally went to the police with the stories of molestation was diagnosed with paranoid schizophrenia. Also, the mental health professional who conducted most of the interviews with the children was accused of using techniques that were suggestive and led children to make up lies about what happened.

I learned that when you go to Tecate, Mexico, you don't dream about having a cold beer after work if you are going to challenge the local police who catch you trespassing.

THE FEELING OF EVIL

"Evil people must spread their evil everywhere."

—*Jane Smiley*

His real first name was Stanley, but they called him "Tookie". Near the end of his life, he was looking for redemption, but that would only come from God. Stanley "Tookie" Williams was executed at California's San Quentin Prison in December of 2005. About one year earlier, I sat face-to-face with this gang killer on death row. It was half an hour of my life I will never forget.

There are two major gangs prowling the streets of Los Angeles, The Bloods and the Crips. "Tookie" Williams founded the Crips. They wear blue bandanas as their visible calling card. Their job is urban terrorism and organized crime. Williams was on death row for killing four people in 1979 during two robberies in the Los Angeles area. These were executions, according to the prosecutor. The victims were all shot at close range with a shotgun. He was convicted and sentenced to death.

I was working at KTNV in Las Vegas as the main evening anchor of Action News. I got a letter from a woman telling me there was a man on death row who was going to be killed by the state of California and that would be a huge loss in the fight against gangs. The woman was the so-called "friend" of Tookie Williams. She was promoting the book he had written in prison. It was a children's book encouraging them to stay away from gangs.

I had seen gang life firsthand in my decade and a half covering the streets of Los Angeles. If there was a way the man who founded the Crips could help kids avoid this violent life, it would be a great story. I pitched it and the news director agreed. We made plans to travel to northern California for a visit to San Quentin.

Arranging to interview someone on death row is a negotiation. First, you bargain to get the inmate or his lawyer. Then, you bargain with prison officials. Tookie Williams, through his "friend", said he would do the interview with me only if I would bring him something very special. He wanted a fresh vegetable sandwich on fresh white bread and a Diet Coke. That was it. It seems on death row you don't get fresh anything very often. It was his luxury and the prison officials said I could bring it in.

The warden refused to let us record the interview. I could not have a video camera or audio recorder. Just a still camera and a note-book, and we were only allowed two photographs that would be taken by a guard. We had no choice but to agree.

I arrived at San Quentin on a day that could be best described as gloomy. I don't know if it was the weather or the feeling inside of me that I was going into a place that was infamous for crime, criminals, and death. It was a feeling of sadness. I wasn't afraid. I was "uncomfortable". Prisons are designed to make you feel that way.

Our prison liaison met us in the lobby. He gave us the rules. We would be led in. The interview would take place in a holding cell. We would sit across a metal table from the inmate. No touching, no hand-shakes, no contact. We had 30 minutes. Williams would have his hands and feet chained to the table. If the guard felt there was any violation of the rules, he would halt the interview immediately.

I had my brown bag carrying the can of Coke and the special vegetable sandwich. They searched it and gave it back to me with a dirty look. It was clear they really didn't want to have to deal with this today. I later learned that guards always worried when prisoners were moved. It's the most dangerous time. Tookie Williams, they said, was potentially dangerous. They still felt he was running the Crips from death row.

I was put in a tiny cell, 6 feet by 6 feet. The floor was concrete, and the walls were steel mesh. The metal table was cold. Then, I heard him coming. A door slammed at the other end of the hall and the sound of the chains was unmistakable. And then, there he was. His eyes were glued to mine through the metal mesh as the guard fumbled with the keys to unlock the cage.

Tookie Williams was a big man with a salt and pepper beard. The door opened and he shuffled in, wearing his prison slippers. He never took his eyes off me.

The guard locked his chains onto a metal loop in the floor and then asked for my camera. He said he would take the pictures when the interview was over. The door slammed shut. I was sitting about 2 feet from a man convicted of killing four people. A man who in one month would be dead himself, as punishment.

I said hello. He said, "Is that my sandwich?" I pushed the bag toward him. As he opened it he said, "Let me eat first. We don't get this kind of food here." I didn't say anything for about 5 minutes while he quietly chewed and sipped the Coke. Finally, he said, "So what do you want from me?" I asked him about his book and why a man convicted of multiple murder and a founder of street gang would now be working to stop violence.

I remember his eyes. I always believed I could see truth in people's eyes. Williams' eyes were cold, as if I were looking at a window shade hiding what was inside. He said all the right things. He said he was innocent. He said he had learned that violence was not the right lifestyle. He said he regretted his gang life. He said prison taught him a new way.

He said it would be a shame to put him to death because he had so much to give and was ready to help solve the gang problem in American cities. He was pleading for his life. But he was doing it with those cold eyes and not much emotion. It was as if he didn't really believe his own words. I don't know if he was telling the truth about what was in his heart. Reporters don't know that we only know what we see and hear and feel.

The interview ended. We could not shake hands. He thanked me for the sandwich. I said thanks for the time. The guard took two pictures of me and Tookie sitting in the cage. He never smiled. He shuffled back to death row.

I remember the deep breath I took when I walked out of San Quentin. I had never "felt" evil before.

A PRAYER AND A $20 BILL

"Trust men and they will be true to you."

—*Ralph Waldo Emerson*

W e can now instantly shoot and send videos around the world from our phones. That was not always the case, which made covering news even more of a challenge. You could have the greatest story and the most amazing video, but no one would see it unless you could get it back to the station in time for the newscast. This story is about taking the ultimate risk/reward to do your job.

Just over four decades ago, in 1977, I was working for WFRV-TV in Green Bay. It was August, and that means summer storms in Wisconsin. I had worked all day and was finally home. Dinner was done and I was watching TV when we saw the tornado warning. It was not to Green Bay yet, but the storm was heading this way. A short time later the phone rang. The night producer told me to get into the station fast! The boss was sending me and a photographer to Wausau, in Marathon County, where a tornado had touched down, causing significant damage. Wausau is about a 90-minute drive from the station. It was going to be a long night. I met Chief Photographer Del Vaughn at the station. He already had the car packed and ready. WFRV had just received its first videotape news camera. We were going to use it tonight.

Let me outline the tools we had to work with to cover this breaking news. There were no cell phones, just phone booths that took a quarter to make a local call. We had no "live" trucks or microwave connections. We had no computers or Wi-Fi links to the station. We were heading out into the night to chase the destruction of a tornado with a camera and a pocket full of quarters. We arrived at the outskirts of Wausau. It was dark. Power was out everywhere, but we didn't see much damage. We drove to the middle of town and took a right turn and saw the flashing lights on the fire trucks and police cars. The tornado had ripped a patch through a residential neighborhood just west of the city.

We got as close as we could, grabbed the gear, and headed down the first street. It was the first time I had witnessed the damage from a tornado. It was eerie. We saw a 2 × 4 turned into a spear that had pierced the side of a metal camper. We also saw a telephone pole turned into a porcupine. When a tornado hits it creates extremely low pressure. That low pressure opens the pores of the wooden telephone poles, and the wind blows sticks and straw into the open slots. When the tornado passes, those holes or pores close quickly, trapping the debris. The pole looked like it had hair! The power of this storm was amazing. We shot video, did interviews, and even told the story of a woman who was found a block from her home still sitting on the mattress from her bedroom. The storm had taken her for a ride. We had great stuff, but no way to get it back to Green Bay and the TV station. The next newscast was the morning broadcast and we had to stay in Wausau until the sun rose.

We took a break and found a truck stop open near the interstate that ran through town. We were frustrated; we could not get to the station and back to Wausau in time for the morning news conference, but we wanted our video to get on the air on the morning show in two hours. There was a truck driver sitting at the next table and I had an idea. I slid into his booth and introduced myself. I asked him where he was heading next. He said, "Green Bay. I am dropping my load at the Procter & Gamble plant on the east side of town." The plant was about 5 minutes from the TV station.

I took a chance. I grabbed the ¾-inch videotape from the machine and handed it to him. This was our only video and if we lost it, we had nothing to show for our long night. I asked him, "Would you drop this at the guard gate when you pull into Procter & Gamble? I will have someone from my station drive over and pick it up."

He smiled and rolled his eyes. "What's in it for me?"

I laid a $20 bill on the top of the tape and said, "You are going that way anyway. Wanna make an easy twenty bucks?" He nodded, grabbed the money and the tape, and he was gone. We watched the big rig and our night's work heading out of the parking lot. Del and I wondered if we would ever see our great video again. I called the station and told them the plan. If the driver did what he agreed to do, WFRV would be the only station with tornado coverage for the morning news programs. We all crossed our fingers.

Del and I went back to work covering the story, and about two hours later I called the newsroom to see if our scheme had worked. The driver did exactly as he promised. The videotape was waiting at the guard shack. Our intern picked it up and our stories and video made the morning broadcast. In the end, this storm had injured 30 people. Luckily, no one died. Winds were clocked at 150 miles per hour.

We had to cover the story and we found out there was always a way. It was risky trusting a truck driver, but what good was a great video if you missed the deadline. For us that night, it was a prayer and a $20 bill that did the trick. When you follow your instincts, you win, most of the time.

AT A LOSS FOR WORDS

"Saying nothing . . . sometimes says the most."

—*Emily Dickinson*

There was only one time when I was on the air in front of a camera when I was literally at a loss for words. I could not believe what I was seeing. The emotions I was feeling were stuck in my throat.

It was April 29th of 1992 and Los Angeles was exploding. Four L.A. police officers were just acquitted in the violent arrest of Rodney King. King was a Black man. The officers were White and tensions in the community were high. I was in the newsroom at KCOP, and we were preparing for trouble. It was late afternoon when the verdict came down from a courtroom in Simi Valley, but it would be South Central L.A. that would become the center of the anger spilling over onto the streets.

We were already hearing about roaming mobs starting fires and shooting. Our crews were sent out and warned to be careful. Some reporter–photographer teams even had armed security guards with them in the trucks.

As the anchor, I knew it would be my and my partner's (Kim Devore) job to try to show people what was happening but not do anything that would fuel the emotional fires that were already burning. The police scanners in the newsroom were cackling, but many of the officers were being told to stay out of the area where the mobs were forming. We believed it was some kind of staging exercise and the officers would move in soon to help regain peace. That never happened.

Our KCOP news helicopter was sent up to help us and our viewers see what was happening on the ground. It was the best and safest way to help tell and show the story. Bob Tur was our reporter and photographer in Chopper 13. I was on the news set with Kim, and our producer told us that Bob had a "live" picture of the intersection of Florence and Normandie Avenues. The live images flashed on our screen in the studio and on the screens of thousands of KCOP viewers.

It was chaos. People were in the streets. Cars were trying to get through the intersection. Some were being stopped and their cars vandalized. Kim and I began narrating the video, telling people what they were seeing, and wondering, out loud and on the air, where the police were.

The next thing we saw was a red truck driving up to the corner and trying to get through. It was a big dump truck with two empty trailers. The men in the street stood in front of the truck. The driver could not move forward. On the air we tried to understand and describe what we were seeing, but there was a bad feeling in the pit of my stomach. I was afraid of what I might see next.

The man in the truck cab was yelling out the window. He was begging for the people blocking him to let him go. They would not. They were Black and angry. They were furious that four White police officers were found not guilty of killing a Black man.

The driver of the red truck was a White man, Reginald Denny. We did not know his name, but we knew he was in danger. As we watched live on television in Los Angeles, Denny was pulled from the cab and four men began beating him. All he could do was put his hands over his face and head. Denny was on his side on the street getting hit and kicked. He was hit with a concrete block and a claw hammer, and one man grabbed a canister that was strapped to the truck and used it to smash Denny in the head.

This was all happening live on television, and we had to find a way to talk to our viewers about what they were seeing too. I was saying things like "We can only hope the police will move in soon or this man is going to be killed." But there were no police. I could not understand why this was happening to an innocent person who was just trying to drive his truck home after a day's work and why the police were not rushing to help him. I was at a loss for words. As Denny lay there in the street bleeding, the live picture from the helicopter staying on the air, I said, "What you have just witnessed live here on KCOP is horrendous. I don't know what more to say." There was nothing more I could say. I sat silently for nearly 30 seconds. Then I saw a man run into the street and up to the truck driver. It was a Black man, that's all we knew, and he was helping Reginald Denny. He took him to his car parked nearby and they were gone.

It was a gut punch that started an 8-hour live broadcast that night. We had live coverage of stores being looted, buildings being burned, pleas from White and Black and Asian store owners to stop the violence, and police refusing to go in and try to curb the rioting.

We had armed guards stationed on the roof of our Hollywood TV studios because the fires and rioting were so close, we could hear the sirens and smell the smoke. I still remember that smell and the feeling of fear. I will also never forget those images that took my words away.

BURIED IN THE SNOW

"The more you can have control over your ego rather than let it run
amuck, the more successful you'll be in all areas of life."

—*Roy T. Bennett*

When you are young and aggressive, there is a feeling nothing can stop you. It's a good quality to have as a journalist, but it can also propel you into dangerous or embarrassing situations. That's what happened in the winter of 1978 while I was working for WTHR in Indianapolis. We knew the big blizzard was coming, but it was just snow and wind and cold, and people in the Midwest can handle it. This, however, was going to be a big storm, predicted to dump several feet of snow pushed by 40-plus-mile-per-hour winds. This one might be different.

I grew up in Wisconsin, so I had seen some big blizzards, and I was ready. The news director put together a coverage plan and we were all asked to sleep at the motel across the street from the WTHR studios so there would be no excuses about us getting to work the next morning when the blizzard would be howling through central Indiana.

Photojournalist Russ Hornickel and I were assigned to roam the streets during the storm looking for people stranded or stuck. The station even rented us a four-wheel drive Jeep to use to keep us from becoming storm victims. Turns out it did not help.

The storm was already howling when we left the station parking lot mid-morning. It had been snowing and blowing all night. Not even the snowplows had been out yet, so the city streets were already buried in almost a foot of snow. Other than a few desperate people walking to a neighborhood market, the city was deserted.

We knew the biggest problem would be the interstate highway that cuts through downtown Indianapolis. It was a major east–west route in the United States and was always jammed with cars and trucks. We pulled off Meridian Street and onto the ramp leading to I-70 heading east. The wind was blowing the snow across the five lanes and piling up along the shoulders. Cars were crawling, trying to stay in the middle. The big rig drivers who decided they were good enough to keep going during the blizzard were slowed to a crawl, making things extra treacherous.

About a mile east of downtown we came upon one of those big trucks. It had jackknifed and part of the trailer was hanging over the edge of the shoulder. Russ and I got out, he grabbed the camera covered with a plastic bag, and we went to the door of the truck and knocked. The driver cracked it open just an inch and growled, "What do you want"? He didn't want to get out of the truck, but he opened the window and I talked with him about the storm and why he kept driving and what he would do now that he's stuck. It was our first victim of the blizzard. In just a few minutes we would be victims, too.

We were feeling pretty good. Our four-wheel drive Jeep was cutting through the snow and kept us going. But the snow was getting thicker, and the wind was getting stronger. We headed south on the outer loop around the city. The assignment desk called and said the governor was activating the National Guard to help rescue people stranded in their cars and trucks. We were told to head to the Holt Avenue exit and go south toward the National Guard staging point at a place called Stout Field.

When we got off the freeway, we came to a wall of snow. The wind had piled a series of drifts across the road. Some were 6 or 7 feet deep. We had about three blocks to get to the entrance gate at Stout Field, where the Guard was mobilizing. The station wanted us to go live as soon as we got there. I looked at Russ and he looked at me. I said, "It's just snow and we have a four-wheel drive Jeep. Let's go." My excitement and adrenaline were pushing us into a very bad decision.

The drifts were higher than the hood of the jeep. We plowed into the first one and made it through. I told Russ to get up ahead of steam and try to hit the second one so we could cut through it. He did and it worked. We headed for the next huge mound of snow and slammed into it. But then, suddenly, the engine died. We tried firing it again and nothing. The Jeep was stuck, and it would not start. The snow was so deep we couldn't even get the doors open. The guy from Wisconsin who bragged about this being just a little snowstorm was now stuck and cold, and a little embarrassed.

We radioed the assignment desk. The assignment editor asked us to hold on. When he came back to the radio, he said there were no tow trucks out and none would go out in this weather. Russ and I pushed the snow away from the doors and got out and tried to push the Jeep. No luck.

A few minutes later the station radioed again. The news director had called the National Guard and it was coming to rescue us! The same people we were sent to interview about storm rescues were now going to rescue us.

With the engine off, it was getting very cold as we waited for our saviors. It was about 20 minutes when we saw a puff of snow in the distance and then another one and another one, and we heard the growl of the engine. The National Guard had sent an armored personnel carrier to get us! It didn't take long. The guardsmen hooked on a chain and pulled us through about six big snowdrifts right into the main entrance at Stout Field. As we were pulled in, some of the troops waiting to leave were smiling and applauding. Yes, they had rescued the media. The same people who were telling everyone to stay home! How embarrassing!

They pulled the Jeep into a warm garage, and we all got out. The captain said, "Let's see why this won't start." He opened the hood, and you could not see the engine. There was snow packed all around the engine right up to the hood! We had been hitting those drifts and driving in the wind and the snow had packed the engine compartment and smothered the engine.

We did our live report. We shared our experience and the anchors made sure to point out that I was bragging about my ability to navigate in winter weather. It was my first professional lesson in humility. When I did the live interview with the National Guard captain, I asked him if he had any advice for drivers right now. He said, "Don't do what you guys just did."

I am not saying I learned that lesson forever.

DON'T EVER ASK A QUESTION

"Patience and trust in the process will lead to extraordinary results."

—*Grant Cardone*

The advice I got was "Never ask the Pope a question!"

In 1987, while at KCBS in Los Angeles, we were preparing for a trip to the Vatican to shoot an eight-part series about the changing Catholic Church. The Pope was coming to the United States later that year, including a stop in Los Angeles. We were working with the press office at the Vatican, hoping to get an audience with Pope John Paul II while we were in Rome. The odds were good, we were told.

One of the rituals when you visit the Vatican as a reporter is a meeting with the Vatican Press Office for an orientation. There are several "official" rules, and some "unofficial" rules the press attaché will never tell you. For instance, you can get access to some secret areas of the Vatican if you make friends with some of the Vatican guards. They are the men who are dressed in the wild costumes and appear to be protecting doors and passageways. They are NOT ceremonial. They are highly trained security agents, but they are also the friendliest people in the Holy City. I worked for CBS News, and we had CBS pens and keychains with us. The Vatican guards loved to get the swag to take home to their children. So, when we wanted access to a secret area, we just gave the guards some of the CBS-marked trinkets and it worked like magic. We were in.

The major "official" rule, I was told, was how to talk to the Pope if we ever got the chance to meet him. Never ask the Pope a question, they said. So how was I supposed to talk with him? The press representative helping us said Pope John Paul II was very open and friendly, but very busy and always meeting people. So, he said, if we got the chance to be face-to-face with him during an audience or while he was blessing people in Vatican Square, just make a statement to him and hope it began a conversation. I call these sport questions. If you listen to a sports reporter talking to athletes after a game, they say, "Your defense really stepped it up today." It's not a question, it's a statement and the player or coach agrees or disagrees and goes on to elaborate. You do the same with the Pope.

On our third day at the Vatican, we were privileged to attend a papal mass in St. Peter's Square. There were thousands of people standing inside the barricades trying to get a glimpse of the Pope. They had been waiting for hours. The press office gave us access to the area near the altar where the Pope would walk and bless people lined up along the railing. We were shoulder-to-shoulder with visitors from all over the world. The Pope was their spiritual leader. Some were crying, just happy they were able to get this close to the man their call their "Father".

Larry Greene, the legendary CBS photojournalist, was next to me on the left as the Pope moved toward us along the railing. Larry had the shot, and I had the opportunity, but I could not ask a question. I had to get the Pope to talk with me and look directly into the camera. As he got closer, I saw that he was reaching out and touching some of the people. When it got to me, I grabbed his hand and looked directly into his eyes. Larry had the camera rolling and we were both just inches from the leader of the Catholic Church. I said, "Holy Father, we are from Los Angeles, California, and the people there are looking forward to your visit in a few months."

He stopped, smiled, and said, "I am truly looking forward to visiting with all of you in Los Angeles. Please give everyone there my blessing. I will be with them soon." He gave us his blessing, let go of my hand, and moved on down the railing. If I had asked a question, I am told, he would not have answered. But, because I made a statement, the Pope was comfortable delivering a message to the viewers I was there representing.

What is interesting, and other reporters will agree, is that when you are in the "moment" and doing your job, you don't think about the consequences or significance of it. We were working hard. We were in a huge crowd. We were trying to make sure we got what we needed to tell the story. I didn't realize how that moment, holding the Pope's hand and talking with him, would stay with me and affect me. I was raised a Catholic, and the Pope was always a mythical figure living in a mystical place called Vatican City. Now, I had met him. I tell my friends that there is something special about a Pope. You do feel you are in the presence of something more than just a leader of men.

I didn't ask the Pope a question. Sometimes you must know the rules and sometimes the rules work for you. And, if you must break the rules, it's always good to be able to say the Pope is your friend.

Pope's US tour KCBS coverage crew

"HAIL SATAN!"

"Big deal. Death always went with the territory. See you in Disneyland".

—*Richard Ramirez, after being sentenced to death*

W hen an inmate in leg chains is led into a courtroom, it is the sound that grabs you before anything else. I still remember the clanking of the metal sliding across the floor as I covered the trial of serial killer Richard Ramirez, the so-called "Night Stalker".

During the mid-1980s, someone was breaking into homes in the Los Angeles area, raping and killing women. It appeared to be random, and that made it more terrifying. People living near freeways were warned to be especially careful. The person doing it was ruthless and brutal and kept getting away. In some cases, the killer would gouge the eyes of his victim. The break-ins all happened at night, so the media began calling him the "Night Stalker". Police said they had very few leads.

I was working as a reporter for KCBS-TV. We were all covering the sexual assaults and killings and the fear that gripped the city and the suburbs. The "Night Stalker" was responsible for 14 killings over 14 months. Finally, in 1988, police captured Richard Ramirez, and when he made his first appearance in a Los Angeles Superior courtroom, I was there. A bizarre case was about to get even crazier.

The day of the arraignment was a media circus. It was the first time the community was going to see the man the police say had been terrorizing them for months. The judges in Los Angeles, at the time, allowed cameras in the courtroom and we were there. It would not take long, and there was not much mystery about what was going to happen. Ramirez would be led in and made to stand behind a glass wall. He would be officially charged with 14 murders, and he would be ordered held with no bail.

Some people in the courtroom that day were relatives of the victims. They, too, wanted to get a glimpse of this man accused of raping, killing, and mutilating their loved ones. The room was packed and hot and buzzing. We heard the lock on the door to the holding cell bang open, and a moment later we saw him. His hair was long and wavy. He looked gaunt. But it was his eyes that were different. They were sinister. The man we had called the "Night Stalker" looked like someone who Hollywood producers could cast as a frightening killer.

The judge came in and asked everyone to come to order. The clerk began reading the charges, and when she finished the judge asked Ramirez, "How do you plead?"

One of his lawyers quickly answered, "Not guilty, your Honor!"

At that moment, Ramirez looked agitated. He raised his left hand, exposing his palm to the packed courtroom, and he yelled, "Hail Satan!"

There was a gasp. The deputies grabbed him and quickly led him from the room and the place was buzzing. I heard people saying, "What was that printed on his hand?"

It was a pentagram. Drawn in ink from a ballpoint pen. A pentagram is an ancient religious symbol adopted by those involved in witchcraft or devil worship. Richard Ramirez had one on his hand in court while yelling, "Hail Satan!" I heard some in the courtroom mutter, "It proves he is the devil."

I remember feeling fear myself. The fear that gripped the community was real and so was what we had just witnessed in a court of law. A man accused of the crime talking about the devil and flashing a symbol to prove he meant it.

I was also there in the same courtroom, months later, when he was found guilty and sent to death row at San Quentin. This is when, for the last time, we heard those leg chains clanking on the tile floor as he was led in. Occasionally, he would turn around in the courtroom and flash an evil look at the reporters sitting behind him. Richard Ramirez lived up to the name we had given him, "The Night Stalker".

IN THE MIDDLE OF A GRIEVING MOB

"We have two ears and one mouth so that we can listen twice as much as we speak."

—*Epictetus*

I was in sixth grade when we got the horrible news that President John F. Kennedy was assassinated. It was the first time I realized the power of television. I was glued to the coverage of an American tragedy, and it ignited my interest in journalism.

Many years later I found myself covering another assassination and drawing comparisons to the Kennedy murder. This time it was in Mexico where there was no holding back the passion or emotion. I have been in the middle of wildfires, riots, and even a KKK cross-lighting but never felt what I felt during this story unfolding on the streets of Mexico City.

It was 1994 and I was the main anchor for KCOP-TV Real News in Los Angeles. The Associated Press bulletin was only one line about an assassination attempt in Tijuana against Mexican presidential candidate Luis Donaldo Colosio. The wounds from two bullets fired at close range during a campaign rally eventually killed the popular candidate. It was a major political and personal story for millions of people on both sides of the border.

We landed in Mexico City for the funeral just 24 hours after the assassination and there were already banners and signs posted on lights posts and walls depicting Colosio's face. Some mourned his death; others were demanding justice. The signs should have been a warning that we were walking into a country where many people were now hurt, angry, and afraid. Our first stories drew comparisons to the feelings of Americans in the days after John Kennedy was shot in Dallas, Texas. The man accused of shooting Colosio had already been captured, and some were linking him to a political conspiracy to affect the upcoming election.

The official memorial ceremony was held at the main offices of Colosio's political party, the Institutional Revolutionary Party, or PRI. Security was tight and the ceremony was closely controlled and planned. But then the day became more chaotic, and I was caught in the middle of it.

We followed the black hearse carrying Colosio's body to a neighborhood on the south side of the city. A small family funeral was planned at a funeral home there. But as we approached the area, we saw the streets jammed with people. The hearse stopped. We jumped out of our rented car and saw the back door of the hearse open. Several men grabbed the flag-draped box, lifted it on their shoulders, and began carrying Colosio's body toward the small funeral home about four blocks away.

The people on the street pressed closer and began chanting, "Colosio, Colosio, Colosio." There were no police, no security patrol, just people wanting to get close to the man they considered their leader. Some of them were crying and reaching to touch the coffin or the colorful Mexican flag that covered it. I looked up, as we struggled through the mob, and saw women standing on balconies, waving handkerchiefs. Tears were streaming down their faces.

Colosio was supposed to be their political savior. He was the candidate promising to speak for them. He was young and handsome and leading in the polls. The people of this neighborhood were saying goodbye, not just to the man but also to their dream. Some were angry. They told me they believed the mayor of Mexico City hired the man to assassinate Colosio. They wanted justice.

Here is the point to this story. I was caught in the middle of a grieving mob, but I did not feel afraid. Instead, I could feel the love these people had for the man and the hope he gave them. I could also feel their frustration and anger. They knew they would never really know who killed him and why. They were powerless again, except for the power of their tears.

We arrived at the funeral home. The casket was taken inside, but the people remained outside. It seemed to be they just wanted to be close to him. They were praying. Colosio was their John Fitzgerald Kennedy. I will never forget the raw emotion I felt that day walking shoulder to shoulder on the streets of Mexico City, listening to people who had their hopes killed by an assassin's bullet. It changed Mexican politics forever. It changed me, just like Kennedy's death changed me and this country.

ON THE NEWS DESK AT KCOP IN LOS ANGELES WITH KIM DEVORE

THE GOVERNMENT WAS LISTENING

"When you're taking chances, you know it's not going to please everybody."

—*Larry Wilmore*

When a mysterious-looking letter arrives and it's clearly from the U.S. government, it usually gets your attention. When I ripped one such open in 1975, it was a warning from the Justice department that my phone conversations were monitored. I really got someone's attention in Washington, just by making a phone call.

I was still in college at the University of Wisconsin–Platteville, but I had an internship at WLUK-TV in Green Bay. It was my Christmas holiday break, and the station needed me to help. It turned out one of the biggest stories in Wisconsin history broke that January of 1975 and I was in the middle of it.

The Menominee Indian reservation was about an hour's drive from Green Bay just outside the town of Shawano. Near the reservation in the town of Gresham was an old ornate stone building, a Roman Catholic novitiate where priests were occasionally training and did their retreats. It was a huge building surrounded by nothing but forest land. It did not belong to the Indian tribe, but on January 1, that didn't matter. The Menominee Warriors Society led by Michael Sturdevant armed themselves and invaded the building and began what would be a 34-day armed occupation of the building. They took six hostages, two of them children.

It was a protest. The Warriors Society arm of the tribe became the activists fighting for the rights of Native Americans. But it was more than a peaceful protest. They had weapons and were threatening to shoot anyone who came close to the building. The Wisconsin governor called up 2000 National Guard troops to surround the place and try to prevent the armed activists from engaging with people in the nearby city of Shawano. It was a standoff. A dangerous one.

Gil Buettner was a veteran reporter and photographer, and he and I left the station on a Saturday heading for Gresham to cover the story that weekend. We drove to the novitiate but could not get close. The Wisconsin State Police and the National Guard soldiers were manning roadblocks. It was cold and clear. The snow was deep. We could not even see the building through the trees. We had no story, yet.

Gil and I decided to head back to the small town of Gresham. We pulled into the parking lot of a small grocery store, and I was going to call the station to discuss our next move with the assignment desk. In 1975 there were no cell phones. We had to find a telephone booth and drop in our dimes and quarters to make a call. Gil was standing with me at the door of the phone booth. He said, "Hey, I have an idea. Let's try something." He grabbed the local phone book. Every booth had one hooked to a chain for cable. He began flipping through the pages and then said, "Here is the number for the novitiate. Let's try to call in to see if anyone answers."

We set up a cassette tape recorder and taped the microphone to the phone earpiece. I attached a microphone to my winter coat and Gil pointed the CP-16 film camera at me as I dialed the number from the phone book. It rang three times, and then a voice. "Hello, who is this?" the man said. I identified myself as a reporter for WLUK and asked him for a name. "This is the General," he said. The General was the name given to Michael Sturdevant, the leader of the Menominee Warriors Society and the man who led the assault on the building. With Gil rolling film and me recording the voice from the phone, I conducted a short interview. He talked about his reasons for the takeover and the resolve of the Native Americans to capture and keep what was theirs.

We had our story. We also had the attention of the U.S. Justice Department, specifically the FBI.

About a month after that phone-booth interview, I got the U.S. government letter. For a journalism student, it was a badge of honor. The federal agents were monitoring the telephone communications in and out of the building and I got caught in the net. Federal law required them to notify me. It was all in the letter. The armed standoff lasted for 34 days and ended peacefully.

I kept the government letter for years. I don't know where it is now. It was a reminder of one of my early victories chasing stories. Thanks, Gil, for the great idea. Take a risk. Make that phone call. You never know who is going to answer and who might be listening.

TOO TIRED TO BE SCARED

"I'd rather regret the things I've done than regret the things I haven't done."

—*Lucille Ball*

I f you have ever been in an emergency landing in a jetliner, you would remember it, right?

Well, I don't.

In 1987, Pope John Paul II came to the United States and began a 7-day tour of 8 U.S. cities. I was chosen by KCBS-TV in Los Angeles to travel with the Pontiff and file reports from each city. It was going to be a grueling work trip with long hours and difficult conditions, but it was also exciting. It was not the first time I had covered the Pope. In fact, earlier in the year we had been to the Vatican to do a preview series on the Catholic church, and I got the chance to meet the Holy Father. That was amazing.

This historic papal trip began in hot and rainy Miami. Each stop had a different theme, but each one had the same general outline. The pope would arrive, meet local government and church officials, and then hold a huge mass for people who had been waiting in line for hours to get near their religious leader. In all, we would end going from

Florida, to South Carolina, to Louisiana and on to San Antonio. Then the trip took us to Phoenix, Los Angeles, San Francisco, and finally, Detroit. Our KCBS team had a spot on the Pope's media plane, so we were on a tight schedule and traveled with him everywhere. It was in New Orleans that I had an experience that I can't remember, but yet will never forget.

The stop in New Orleans was a tough one. The Pope had his event at an arena in the suburbs, but our "live" shot reporting location was downtown on the roof of an old brewery. By the time we finished it was long after midnight. We didn't get any sleep because the flight leaving for San Antonio was leaving in just a few hours. We made it and I collapsed into my seat on the TWA L1011. I immediately fell sound asleep.

When I woke up in a sleepy haze and looked around the plane, it was nearly empty, and we weren't moving. We were on the tarmac! I glanced to my right and saw one of the other reporters sitting in a seat across the aisle and asked, "Where are we?"

She said, "New Orleans."

I was confused. I had been asleep for nearly 3 hours, and we were still on the ground in Louisiana and the rest of the reporters and crew on board were gone. We should have been on the ground in San Antonio.

I got up and went to the front of the plane and found some other reporters playing cards. I said, "What are we doing here?"

One of them looked at me puzzled and said, "Did you sleep through that?" He told me that during takeoff from New Orleans, the plane started shaking and the pilot declared an emergency. He said, "We made one circle in the air and landed hard. It was an emergency landing!" He told me it would be another hour for repairs before we could try to take off again.

I slept through the entire emergency landing! I was too tired to be scared. So, now I tell the story about my close call during my coverage of the Pope, but I don't remember any of it. We took off again, heading for Texas. There were many parts of that exciting assignment I remember, but I regret being too tired to remember this one.

(BTW . . . I also covered the Pope visiting the United States in 1979 while working for WTHR in Indianapolis, and again in 1993 while working for KCOP in Los Angeles.)

SNEAKING BACK INTO THE U.S.

"What I wouldn't give for a little old smuggling job."

—*Katherine McIntyre*

No, I did not go to Mexico to buy drugs and smuggle them into the U.S., but I was in the car when it happened.

Have you ever heard of Laetrile? It's a naturally occurring drug found in many plants, but mostly found in the seeds of apricots, almonds, apples, peaches, and plums. Some people believe it helps cure cancer. The federal government regulators do not. But you can get laetrile treatments and buy the drug in Mexico. Some people risk a lot going there and getting it. For many it's their last hope in their battle against cancer and that is where this story begins. It ends at the U.S.–Mexico border in a car surrounded by drug agents.

I was working as a reporter/photographer for WFRV-TV in Green Bay, Wisconsin. It was my first job after graduating from college and I was learning something new every day. The news director came to me and told me I was going to accompany our main anchor, Dan Spaulding, on a trip to California with a side trip into Mexico. He would do the reporting and I would shoot the film: Yes, it was film.

WHAT YOU SAW...AND WHAT YOU DIDN'T

A woman from a small town south of Green Bay had been bat-
tling cancer for years and the doctors told her there was little more they
could do. She had heard about the controversial laetrile drug available
south of the border and was going to try it. We were going along.

Dan and I flew to San Diego and rented a car and drove south.
We pulled into a small motel in San Ysidro and met the woman and
her husband. The plan was to spend the night there and head south
across the border in the morning. I would shoot film of her going into
the clinic and, if the doctors would allow it, record her getting the
treatments. Then, we would simply head back to the U.S. and do our
final interview with her back at the motel.

The next morning, we crossed into Mexico. It was my first time
there. I was excited and focused. I didn't want to let our main anchor
down, and I wanted to help tell this woman's story the best way I
could. I enjoyed shooting the video. It was another way I could learn
great storytelling.

It all went as planned. The woman got her laetrile treatments at
the Tijuana clinic. Then she went into a private meeting with the clinic
doctors and Dan, and I waited outside near the car that the couple had
rented. When they came out, we piled in. I was sitting in the back seat
with Dan and all our gear. The husband and wife were in the front seat.

When we got to the border, we knew there would be questions
about the TV gear, but it was just routine, so we were not worried.
However, the mood suddenly changed. The U.S. border agents called
for assistance and started asking the couple more questions about the
reason for their visit. The couple just said it was a pleasure trip and they
were on vacation. The agents, seemingly, were not buying it.

They ordered all of us out of the car and the man was asked to
open the trunk. The search of the car lasted about 5 minutes. They

kept asking us if we bought any prescription drugs or marijuana. They found nothing. So, we all got back in and headed north into the United States. When we pulled into the motel parking lot and got out, we decided to do the interview with the woman on a picnic table next to the building. As we sat down and began setting up our gear, I asked the woman if she was worried about the extra search we endured at the border. We were laughing about it by then because the tension was gone. But she said she was very worried, and she showed me why.

She opened the zipper on her jacket and unbuttoned her blouse. She had on a cotton undershirt and taped to the undershirt were small vials of liquid. It was laetrile. I counted them; 16 vials of a drug which was illegal to transport into the United States were hidden under her clothing. She had not told us she was going to bring any of the drug into the country. We only thought she was going to get treatments in Mexico.

I looked at Dan and he looked at me, and we realized how close we had come to being detained, maybe arrested, for conspiracy to smuggle illegal drugs across the border. The woman was apologetic. Not for smuggling drugs but for putting us in danger. She told us she deliberately kept it a secret so we would not be afraid. Even her husband driving the car didn't know. She was desperate to find something to fight her cancer, even if it meant risking arrest. It all became part of our story.

I am glad those federal agents didn't ask to search her. It was another very close call.

(Postscript: Unfortunately, maybe predictably, the drugs did not work. She died of cancer about 3 months after our trip to Mexico.)

YOU GOTTA HAVE TRUST

"If you're not living on the edge, you're taking up too much space."

—*Jim Whittaker*

When you are 1,000 feet off the ground, in a fog, strapped into a helicopter, and trying to make a deadline, you gotta have trust.

In 1978, I was working at WTHR-TV in Indianapolis and was assigned to cover a court case that led to the demise of an iconic American automobile. What became known as the Ford Pinto trial was underway in a tiny courthouse in a small town in northern Indiana. The best way to get there and back from Indianapolis daily was by helicopter. That way I could meet my deadlines and have the most complete coverage.

Eighteen-year-old Judy Ulrich was driving a 1973 Ford Pinto. Her sister and cousin were in the car with her. They were stopped on the side of the road when a van plowed into the back of the Pinto, and it burst into flames. All three burned and died. Ford issued an immediate recall, and Pinto owners were demanding answers about the car's safety.

A grand jury then did something that had never been done before. It indicted the Ford Motor Company on three counts of reckless homicide. Ford hired famous lawyer James Neal, and the media circus was on. The trial was moved to Winamac, Indiana—population, 2,400. Every motel room within miles of the tiny northern Indiana town was booked for months. So, we were forced to make the commute via helicopter daily.

On the final day of the trial, Ford was acquitted of the murder charges and the lawyers made their statements on the courthouse steps. I was there with my photojournalist partner, and we jumped in our car heading for the farmers field just outside of town where our WTHR helicopter was waiting. This was not the first time we had made this trip back to Indianapolis, but this time would be different. I had to start writing my script, so we could begin editing our video as soon as we landed and returned to the TV station. I was sitting in the front seat next to the pilot as we lifted off the field and began heading south for the 45-minute flight.

About 5 minutes into the flight, I noticed the sky getting darker. The fog was closing in. The pilot was forced to fly closer to the ground to stay under the haze. Suddenly, it got so thick he said to us, "We are going to need to land; we can't go much lower."

I panicked. "We can't make our deadline if we land here," I said. The route south was mostly farming fields. Flat and uninteresting, but in those fields were huge high-tension power lines carrying electricity back and forth across the state. Those power lines were in our way, and because of the fog, we couldn't see them.

The pilot said to me there was a way, but it was risky. I would have to use a map showing the location of the power lines and warn the pilot about 100 yards before reaching each of them. That way he could stop the chopper in midair, increase altitude to go over the power lines, and then drop down again on the other side below the fog. It was like crawling with a blindfold in. One wrong decision and the chopper would be tangled in the lines and come crashing down. I said, "Let's do it."

One by one, we carefully hopscotched over the powerlines. I was terrified. I could not see anything in the fog, and I really couldn't look because I had to focus on the map and my critical warnings to the pilot. Sometimes we would get to within feet of the power cables before the pilot was able to pull up and crawl over the top of them. The usual 45-minute flight took nearly 90 minutes, but we made it.

When you are doing something risky, you rarely think about the consequences. It's only afterwards that reality hits home.

I made my deadline. The story was on the air. I did my job, but later I realized that one miscalculation by me or the pilot could have been a disaster. We can all hope that when we do risky things, we learn from them. I don't think I did. It would not be the last time I took a dangerous risk to get a story.

THE SOUND OF DESPAIR

"In an endless silence even screams sound silent."

—*Dejan Stojanovic*

One of the hardest things I have experienced so far in my journalism career is waiting to find out if someone missing is dead or alive. My first taste of this moment came in 1975, at the beginning of my career, in a muddy parking lot on the west side of the Fox River in Green Bay, Wisconsin.

The metropolitan sewer district was digging a tunnel. It was a huge undertaking. Drilling hundreds of feet straight down and then horizontally underneath the Fox River and then up to the surface again on the other side. It was one of those projects that mostly went unnoticed until something went wrong. And on a rainy Monday morning in May, something went very wrong.

The men digging this tunnel were a combination of local men and construction workers from around the state hired to come here until the job was done. They were always aware of the risk of digging underground, but they took precautions, and the money was good.

The tunnel they were digging would carry a simple but large sewer pipe to help support the growing population of the city. It was the Packer football team that put this city on the map, but it was the paper industry that kept growing the population.

I was new to the newsroom at WFRV-TV. I had just graduated from college, and this was my first full-time job as a reporter. On this Monday morning when I arrived in the newsroom, I got my assignment right away. There was an explosion underground. Four men were trapped. Rescuers were trying to reach them. They are staging a command post on the west side of the river.

My thoughts were scrambled. How was I going to cover a story that was happening hundreds of feet underground in a tunnel under a river? I, remarkably, wasn't thinking about the lives of the trapped men. It seemed ridiculous that they would not be brought out alive. It was my first story that involved the potential for death. My mind wasn't ready to grasp the possibility. I was learning. I didn't know they could build a tunnel under a river. I didn't know about methane gas and its dangers. I was struggling to tell the entire story and I nearly missed the human story that was about to unfold over the next 3 days.

The soil under the riverbed had not been disturbed for thousands, maybe millions, of years. People who dig in this environment are always worried about finding pockets of methane gas. You can't smell it, and that makes it more dangerous. The workers, I know now, place detectors in the tunnel where they are digging to warn them of danger. On this Monday morning, the detectors apparently didn't work. The gas built up and something sparked a huge underground blast. The men were trapped. They could not get out and the rescuers could not get to them, and no one knew if they were even still alive.

The men were all from Wisconsin, but they were not from Green Bay. At the first news briefing by the fire chief, he refused to release their names but said rescuers were doing all they could to reach them and bring them out safely. We had no reason to believe that was NOT going to happen. But it didn't. Communication with the men had been cut off and the first firefighters who went into the muddy tunnel came back dirty and frustrated. There was no easy way in, so the decision was made to dig a second tunnel to try to get air to the trapped men. But it was risky. There could be another explosion.

By day two, reality set in. These men might already be dead. I had been focusing on stories about the process and didn't really put myself in the shoes of those men or their families. That changed when a fire chief's car pulled into the command post and a woman, and two children got out. Reporters and photographers crowded around them. The chief pushed us away. They were led to the mouth of the tunnel opening and the captain leading the rescue effort talked with them for about 5 minutes. The woman handed the captain an envelope. He put it in a plastic bag.

When the woman and the two boys turned and walked away, we started walking toward them. It was clear they were "family", and this was where the story changed for me. We pushed the microphones toward her face. She looked confused and in shock. She said she just wanted her husband out alive. She cried. The note in the envelope was for her husband trapped in the tunnel if they could get to him. She said, "It simply says I love you."

The next two days were a blur of more rain, mud, anticipation, despair, and more tears. More family members arrived. Volunteer construction workers from all over the state came to help dig that second tunnel into the main one, hoping to find the men alive and get them some air. When they finally broke through on day three, they confirmed the worst. The men were dead. The explosion didn't kill them. The air ran out.

It was my first story involving tragic death. I will never forget the sound of the crying when the fire chief went to the window of the van where family members were waiting and told them the news. It's a sound of despair I hear in my head even today.

THE NOTE BEHIND THE PHOTOGRAPH

"The beauty of the world, which is so soon to perish, has two edges,
one of laughter, one of anguish, cutting the heart asunder."

—*Virginia Woolf*

Sometimes things are not what they appear to be. Sometimes you find a last-minute twist that changes a story, changes a life, or changes a family. I found this out while covering the story of a missing girl in May of 1977.

Oconto, Wisconsin, is a town about an hour north of Green Bay, and the sheriff's deputies there were looking for a teenaged girl who had disappeared. Her parents said she didn't come home from school one afternoon and they had not heard from her. It had been 48 hours, and everyone was desperate to find her.

I was a reporter at WFRV-TV in Green Bay, and I was sent there to tell the story of the disappearance and the active search for the girl. I arrived in Oconto and went right to the sheriff's office. We talked with the investigators. One of them told me they had no clues. "This was not the kind of girl to just run away," he said. They were worried she had been kidnapped, but there was no evidence of that either. It was a real mystery.

This was 1977. There was no internet or social media. There was no digital trail that investigators could follow. She had disappeared, seemingly, into thin air and I knew I had to do one of the most difficult things a journalist must do. I had to knock on the door of the family home and ask, not only for information but also to try to get a photograph of the missing girl so I could put it on TV and, maybe, help find her.

It was a small house about two blocks from the river that ran through town. The street was lined with big trees, and I remember as I parked out front that the roses on the bushes around the front porch were beautiful. There were four wooden steps leading to a small front porch. The door was a metal screen door with a white wooden door behind it. I took a deep breath and knocked and waited. About a minute later a woman came to the door.

I introduced myself. "Hi, sorry to bother you. I am a reporter for Channel 5 in Green Bay, and I am working on a story that might help find your daughter." The woman looked down and told me she was her mother. Just then a man appeared behind the woman. It was the father, and both were now talking to me. They told me how confused they were. They could not believe she would run away. She was only 13 years old. There were no tears, just confused and desperate looks on their faces.

I said, "I would help if I could get a photograph of your daughter. I could put it on TV tonight and maybe someone will recognize her. It could help the deputies who are looking for her." They looked at each other and the mother agreed. They asked me to wait on the front porch.

They returned together. The mother was in tears. She was holding a crumpled piece of paper, and the father was holding a picture frame.

In the frame was a photo of their missing daughter. I said, "Why are you crying? I am sorry."

The mother looked up at me and said, "When we went to get the picture, I found this." My little girl killed herself, she said. "She left us this note and we just found it."

I didn't ask what was in the note. The mother and father said I had to go, and I did. I went back to the sheriff's department and told them what had happened. Later that day, they found the girl's body in the river just a block from her home.

The story that day had started with mystery and hope. It ended with tragedy and heartbreaking closure. After all these years I can still see the confused anguish on the face of that mother who had just found out her little girl was dead, and she found out because I had asked for a picture.

THE BIG ONE THAT GOT AWAY

"Don't give up on your dreams, or your dreams will give up on you."

—*John Wooden.*

One of the ways we found stories to chase was by scouring the small-town weekly newspapers from all over Wisconsin. Each community had its own publication filled with school lunch menus, library hours, obituaries, and feature stories about their colorful residents. One morning in 1974, while working at WLUK-TV in Green Bay, I found a story I just didn't believe, but I found out that it really was all about "believing."

The headline in the *Omro Herald* was "Local Man Won't Give Up Search for Giant Catfish". Frank Tucker told his story to the local reporter about the day over a year ago when he was fishing one morning in his sun-bleached old boat in the pond behind his neighbor's barn. Frank said he had never seen a catfish as big as the one on the end of his line. "It wasn't a fighter," he said, "but it was huge." He explained how he rowed the boat toward the shore as he held the fishing pole pinned to the bottom of the boat with his work boot. Just as he got the giant catfish within 15 feet of the crumbling dock, there was a "swoosh" and the big fish got spooked. The thrashing, he said, ripped the hook from the fish's mouth and it was gone. Frank said he sat there alone in the morning sun thinking, *No one is going to believe me.* So, right there and then he made a pledge. He would come back every day and try to catch it again to prove he wasn't crazy.

As I read his story in the newspaper, I knew I had to visit Frank and find out what really drove him to catch a fish he claimed he once had on the end of his fishing pole. He was a character. My instincts told me he had something to teach me.

Two days later I was on my way, early on a Thursday morning. I made the turn off Highway 41 in Oshkosh and headed west. It is farm country, but many of the farms are gone, having been replaced by new houses. Two more turns on those country roads and I saw Frank's mailbox. He said I couldn't miss it. Someone had carved a giant catfish with a mouth that opened for the mail.

Frank met me in the driveway, and I grabbed my camera and microphone from the trunk. He wanted me to meet his wife, Betty. She came to the door with a brown paper bag filled with sandwiches and those small bags of Lay's potato chips. She said we would get hungry out there on the pond. She squeezed Frank's hand, looked at me with a sly smile, and said, "Good luck, men."

It was a short, quarter-mile walk down to the pond that I discovered did not have a name. It was just a pond behind the barn of a farmer who had died long ago. Another farmer who lived miles away now leased the land around it.

Frank kept his old rowboat tied to a dilapidated dock on the east side of the pond. "No one ever bothers it," he said. "Who would want this old thing anyway." It was true. I was surprised the boat would even float.

We loaded our lunch, his fishing tackle, and my camera gear into it and he began slowly rowing. We didn't say anything for about

5 minutes. I just sat there enjoying the sunshine. He stopped rowing and said, "This could be the day." I put the camera on my shoulder and clipped a microphone on Frank's fishing vest while he set up his pole and his bait. He slipped a big piece of bacon fat on the end of that giant hook and tossed it overboard. If that huge catfish was hungry, it had a feast ready.

Frank told me the story again about that day when he hooked the monster fish. It was filled with details. He pointed to the spot where he first felt the tug on the pole and then how the fish kept moving and pulling the rowboat. It was going to be a great story. The light was beautiful, and Frank was a great talker.

He, again, told me he would love to catch that fish again because he wanted to prove to his friends it was not just another big fish story. You could see he loved the hunt, and he loved the pond, and he loved being out in the fresh air.

He changed the bait several times in two hours. I shot more video of the pond and the cars driving by. I found out more about Frank's life. How he met his wife Betty and how he fought in World War II. At lunchtime we ate our sandwiches.

At 1 o'clock we had not had a bite. Frank declared that fish would never bite in the afternoon, so he began packing up his gear. As we walked back to the house, he apologized for not giving me a good story by catching the fish. I told him it was OK, and that it was still a good story about his life and his mission to catch it someday. At the house, Betty greeted us again and I asked Frank to call me when he caught the fish. I wanted a picture of it to follow up.

The story aired the next day on WLUK Channel 11 in Green Bay. It was fantastic. My boss loved it, and some viewers even called to congratulate us on doing the story. We got letters from people suggesting what special bait Frank should use to get his big fish.

About a month later I found a pink phone message slip on my desk when I arrived one morning. It said that Frank's wife, Betty, had called. I was excited because I was hoping Frank had gotten his fish. I was excited to see it and see his face, beaming. I dialed the number and Betty answered. My voice was filled with energy as I said, "Hi, Betty! Did Frank get his fish?!"

She said, "Well, no, Frank did not catch that catfish. Frank is gone. He died three weeks ago." My heart sank. She said, "He died in his sleep, probably dreaming about that fish."

I expressed my sympathy, but I could tell Betty had more to say. I asked her if she was sorry Frank didn't keep his promise to catch that big old catfish he once had on the line in the tiny pond. She said, "Ross, there was never a real fish. But that make-believe fish kept my husband alive. It was the hope he had every day that his fantasy would come true, and that kept him moving and living and dreaming."

I realized that even for Frank, it was never about the fish. It was about hope. He believed his own story about that big fish, because if didn't he would quit living. It was his way. Betty said, "Thank you, Ross, for letting Frank share his story." We hung up.

Now, when I go fishing, I sometimes think of Frank. Even if there is no fish on the end of my line at the end of my day, there is always hope for the next day. Sometimes the stories we cover are not as simple as an old man, an old boat, a small pond, and a big fish story.

FINAL REFLECTIONS

"Life can only be understood backwards; but it must be lived forwards."

—*Soren Kierkegaard*

Now that my five decades of chasing stories is over, I have had time to reflect on everything I saw, everyone I met, those I worked with, and those who worked against me.

The stories in this book are just a handful of the stories I covered during my career. I don't have all the scripts and the videos anymore, but I have lists and lists of "slug" lines and dates. As I look over them, lots of memories come rushing back.

All reporters have stories about their stories. They have met unusual and famous people. In that way mine were not unique. What is unique is how each of us reacts to and grows after each one we encounter.

There are many stories I did not put in this book. I chose the ones that had the most impact on me and the ones you might recognize.

Also, I did not do this alone. Journalism, often, is a team effort. I want to thank the managers, researchers, producers, photographers, editors, artists, and production crew members. They are all living this life with us.

Finally, don't blame the messenger. Many news consumers today believe journalists are the enemy. Are there bad and unethical journalists? Of course. Identify them and ignore them. Find the ones who show and tell you the truth. Not the truth you want to hear, but the truth you need to hear. Challenge yourself to be open to something you don't believe. Get the facts from a journalist or two or three and then make up your mind.

Democracy can't survive without journalists. There is no such thing as a "citizen" journalist, just like there is no such thing as a "citizen" doctor or lawyer. You want professionals as the gatekeepers of the truth.

There is much you see every hour on TV or online, but there is a lot you don't see. It's the human side of life and journalism.

ON THE STREETS AT THE 2016 GOP CONVENTION
IN CLEVELAND